LORD HEAR

☨ OUR PRAYER

Prayer is the light of the soul, giving us true knowledge of God. Prayer is a precious way of communicating with God, it gladdens the soul and gives repose to its affections.

St. John Chrysostom (ca. 347-407)

LORD HEAR

✠ OUR PRAYER

Revised Edition
compiled by
William G. Storey, D.M.S.
Professor Emeritus of Liturgy
University of Notre Dame

and

Thomas McNally, C.S.C.
Associate Pastor
St. Clement's Parish, Hayward, California

ave maria press Notre Dame, IN

Nihil Obstat: David Burrell, C.S.C
            Censor Deputatus
Imprimatur: William E. McManus
            Bishop of Fort Wayne-South Bend
First published October 1978
International Standard Book Number: 0-87793-684-6
© 1978, 2000 by Ave Maria Press, P.O. Box 428, Notre Dame, Indiana 46556
Printed and bound in the United States of America.
Cover and text design by Brian C. Conley
Illustrations by Ivan Mestrovic (see p. 413)

The copyright acknowledgments which begin on page 387 constitute a continuation of this copyright page.

Lord hear our prayer / compiled by William G. Storey and Thomas McNally.
        p.   cm.
Rev. ed.
Includes bibliographical references and index.
ISBN 0-87793-684-6
    1. Catholic Church Prayer-books and devotions—English
I. Storey, William George, 1923-   .   II. McNally, Thomas.
BX2130.L67   2000
242'.802—dc21   99-41019
                                                       CIP

Contents

Preface

It's no secret that we live in a frantic age; and the pace seems to quicken day by day instead of slowing down. Some psychologists are wondering if human beings can accept and absorb all the changes that our technological society calls on us to make. How much can we take before we fly to pieces?

That's why it's so important for us at times to "idle down," to put the brakes on activity. Wise men and women, whether believers or not, recognize this fact and find time for stillness and reflection in various ways.

And we who believe in the loving Father, and the Son he sent, and the promise of the Holy Spirit, see a need not simply for stillness but for prayer. After all, our lives are not our own but God's, and prayer is our fumbling attempt to affirm this.

By that I don't mean to imply that prayer is simply a problem-solving device, a selfish way to make our lives more bearable. Above all, it is our way to praise and thank the Father for all he is and all he has done.

Furthermore, as Thomas Merton suggests, we are not talking here about simply a private enterprise. Silence, solitude, and prayer are not private projects, says Merton, but belong to the people with whom we live and work. Not only that, but through faith, my prayer puts me in touch with all those millions whom I shall never meet but for whom I pray daily, including those ravaged by poverty, grief, and injustice.

In some mysterious way my prayer today is not simply "mine" but belongs to the whole community; I am comforted by the knowledge that your prayer has room in it for me! There's an expression in Latin—*Oremus pro invicem*—which says it all: Let us pray for each other!

Because of the tremendous importance of prayer in our day, I'm delighted to see this book emanate from the University of Notre Dame. In the 1960s and early 1970s new prayer books were hardly in large supply. There were many reasons for this, including the inevitable uncertainties and changes following the great Second Vatican Council.

My hope, and the hope of the editors and publishers, is that this book will help put prayer in focus again for thousands of Christians; and that it will put them back in touch with the rich Christian tradition of prayer. Furthermore, our hope is that the book will help move

Christians forward in their prayer life, because prayer is not static but dynamic, and cannot be limited to a particular style or time.

The Lord put it best: "Out of his storehouse, the home-owner brought forth things both new and old" (Mt 13:52). The editors have reached into that storehouse and rummaged around for the best in prayers both old and new. I think they have succeeded remarkably well, and I hope you will agree with me after sampling *Lord Hear Our Prayer*.

Oremus pro invicem
Theodore M. Hesburgh, C.S.C.
President Emeritus, University of Notre Dame

> *Prayer is the means whereby we rightly understand the fullness of joy that is coming to us.*
>
> **Julian of Norwich (1342-1416)**

1. Everyday Prayers

The Lord's Prayer

Jesus was an example of prayer for his disciples and taught them how to pray and what to say.

[Jesus] was praying in a certain place, and after he had finished, one of his disciples said to him,
"Lord, teach us to pray, as John [the Baptist] taught his disciples." He said to them, "When you pray, say:

Father [Abba], hallowed be your name.
Your kingdom come.
Give us each day our daily bread.
And forgive us our sins,
    for we ourselves forgive
    everyone indebted to us.
And do not bring us to the time of trial.
(Luke 11:1-4, NRSV)

Matthew's gospel has another version of the Lord's Prayer:

Our Father in heaven,
hallowed be your name.
Your kingdom come.
Your will be done,
on earth as it is in heaven.
Give us this day our daily bread.
And forgive us our debts,
as we also have forgiven our debtors.
And do not bring us to the time of trial,
but rescue us from the evil one.
(Matthew 6:9-13, NRSV)

The early Church added an appropriate conclusion to these New Testament versions :

For the kingdom, the power, and the glory are yours now and for ever. Amen.

The Lord's Prayer is the most basic of all our forms of prayer. Many Catholics learned the traditional form of the Lord's Prayer in these words:

Our Father, who art in heaven,
hallowed be thy Name;
thy kingdom come;
thy will be done on earth
as it is in heaven.

Give us this day our daily bread;
and forgive us our trespasses
as we forgive those who trespass
    against us;
and lead us not into temptation,
but deliver us from evil.
For thine is the kingdom and the power
    and the glory for ever and ever. Amen.

The following is the approved Roman Catholic version in its modern form:
Our Father in heaven,
    hallowed be your Name,
    your kingdom come,
    your will be done,
        on earth as in heaven.
Give us today our daily bread.
Forgive us our sins
    as we forgive those who sin against us.
Save us from the time of trial
    and deliver us from evil.
For the kingdom, the power and the glory are yours,
    now and for ever. Amen.

Hail Mary

The angel Gabriel taught us the second most important Catholic daily prayer, the "Hail Mary," when he saluted the Virgin Mary and announced the beginning of our salvation (Luke 1:28). Her cousin Elizabeth, the mother of John the Baptist, "filled with the Holy Spirit" added the second part to our prayer when she exclaimed: "Blessed are you among women, and blessed is the fruit of your womb" (Luke 2:42). The Church added the final part of the "Hail Mary," the name of Jesus, and "Holy Mary, Mother of God, pray for us sinners, now and at the hour of our death. Amen."

Here is its modern form:

Hail, Mary, full of grace,
the Lord is with you.
Blessed are you among women,
and blessed is the fruit of your womb, Jesus.
Holy Mary, Mother of God, pray for us sinners,
    now and at the hour of our death. Amen.

Apostles' Creed

To these fundamental prayers we add the Apostles' Creed composed by the early Roman Church for the baptism of its adult converts:

I believe in God, the Father almighty,
    creator of heaven and earth.

I believe in Jesus Christ, his only Son, our Lord.
He was conceived by the power of the Holy Spirit
    and born of the Virgin Mary.

He suffered under Pontius Pilate,
> was crucified, died, and was buried.
He descended to the dead.
On the third day he rose again.
He ascended into heaven,
> and is seated at the right hand of the Father.
He will come again to judge the living and the dead.

I believe in the Holy Spirit,
> the holy catholic Church,
> the communion of saints,
> the forgiveness of sins,
> the resurrection of the body,
> and the life everlasting. Amen.

After the *Creed* come the great acts of praise of the Most Holy Trinity: the *Doxology*, the *Gloria in Excelsis*, and the *Te Deum*.

The Doxology

Glory to the Father, and to the Son,
> and to the Holy Spirit:
as it was in the beginning, is now,
> and will be for ever. Amen.

Gloria in Excelsis

Glory to God in the highest
    and peace to his people on earth.

Lord God, heavenly King,
almighty God and Father,
    we worship you, we give you thanks,
    we praise you for your glory.

Lord Jesus Christ, only Son of the Father,
Lord God, Lamb of God,
you take away the sin of the world:
    have mercy on us;
you are seated at the right hand of the Father:
    receive our prayer.

For you alone are the Holy One,
you alone are the Lord,
you alone are the Most High,
    Jesus Christ,
    with the Holy Spirit,
    in the glory of God the Father. Amen.

Te Deum Laudamus

You are God: we praise you;
You are the Lord: we acclaim you;
You are the eternal Father:
All creation worships you.

To you all angels, all the powers of heaven,
Cherubim and Seraphim, sing in endless praise:
    Holy, holy, holy Lord, God of power and might,
    heaven and earth are full of your glory.

The glorious company of apostles praise you.
The noble fellowship of prophets praise you.
The white-robed army of martyrs praise you.

Throughout the world the holy Church
        acclaims you:
    Father of majesty unbounded,
    your true and only Son, worthy of all worship,
    and the Holy Spirit, advocate and guide.

You, Christ, are the king of glory,
the eternal Son of the Father.
When you became man to set us free
you did not spurn the Virgin's womb.

You overcame the sting of death
and opened the kingdom of heaven to all believers.

You are seated at God's right hand in glory.
We believe that you will come, and be our judge.

Come, then, Lord, and help your people,
bought with the price of your own blood,
and bring us with your saints
to glory everlasting.

Finally, there are the daily devotions to the Blessed Virgin Mary: *The Angelus* during most of the year, and the *Regina Caeli* during Eastertide. Most churches ring bells for these prayers at 6 a.m., noon, and 6 p.m.

The Angelus

The angel of the Lord brought the message to Mary,
—and she conceived by the Holy Spirit.
Hail, Mary....

I am the Lord's humble servant.
—May it happen to me as you have said.
Hail, Mary....

And the Word was made flesh,
—and dwelt among us.
Hail, Mary....

Pray for us, O holy Mother of God,
—that we may become worthy of the
promises of Christ.

Let us pray:

Pour forth, O Lord,
your grace into our hearts,
that we to whom the incarnation of Christ your Son
was made known by the message of an angel,
may by his passion and cross
be brought to the glory of his resurrection;
through the same Christ our Lord.
—Amen.

Regina Caeli

Joy fill your heart, O Queen most high, alleluia!
Your Son who in the tomb did lie, alleluia!
Has risen as he did prophesy, alleluia!
Pray for us, Mother, when we die, alleluia!

Text: *Regina caeli*, Latin, twelfth century, trans. James Quinn, S.J. *Praise for All Seasons* (Kingston, NY: Selah Publishing, 1994), p. 97.

Rejoice and be glad, O Virgin Mary, alleluia!
—For the Lord has truly risen, alleluia!

Let us pray:

God our Father,
you give joy to the world

by the resurrection of your Son,
    our Lord Jesus Christ.
Through the prayers of his Mother,
    the Virgin Mary,
bring us to the happiness of eternal life.
We ask this through Christ our risen Lord.
—Amen.

One of the most ancient Christian customs, inherited from the Jews, is that of saying grace before and after meals. The origin of the Eucharist lies in Jewish meal prayers and every meal accompanied by thanksgiving to the giver of all good things can be regarded as a kind of eucharist. It is at table together in fellowship and prayer that we are most a family. The following forms of grace are basic and may be supplemented by a Bible reading or by seasonal prayers taken from other sections of this book.

Grace Before Meals

All living things look to you
    to give them their food in due season.
You give it, they gather it up:
    you open your hand, they have their fill.
Glory to the Father, and to the Son,
    and to the Holy Spirit:
as it was in the beginning, is now,
    and will be for ever. Amen.

Bless us, + O Lord, and these your gifts
   which we are about to receive
   from your bounty,
   through Christ our Lord.
—Amen.

Grace After Meals

Let all the works of the Lord bless the Lord,
   and his children shall praise him for ever.
Glory to the Father, and to the Son,
   and to the Holy Spirit:
as it was in the beginning, is now,
   and will be for ever. Amen.

We give you thanks, almighty God,
   for these and all your blessings;
   you live and reign for ever and ever. Amen.

May the souls of the faithful departed
   through the mercy of God rest in peace.
—Amen.

Another precious Jewish custom inherited by us through Jesus and the Apostles is the habit of daily morning and evening prayer. Whether they are longer or shorter, prayers to open and close the day are essential to the Christian life.

A Brief Morning Prayer

Hymn

Now that the daylight fills the sky
We lift our hearts to God on high,
That he, in all we do or say,
Would keep us free from harm today:

Would guard our hearts and tongues from strife,
From anger's din would hide our life,
From evil sights would turn our eyes,
Would close our ears to vanities.

So we, when this new day is gone
And night in turn is drawing on,
With conscience by the world unstained
Shall praise his Name for victory gained.

To God the Father and the Son
And Holy Spirit, three in one,
Be endless glory as before
The world began, so evermore.
—Amen.

Text: *Iam lucis orto sidere*, Latin, eighth century, trans. John Mason Neale
(1818-1866), alt.

Psalm 100   A Hymn of Praise

Sing to the Lord, all the world!
Worship the Lord with joy;
come before him with happy songs!

Acknowledge that the Lord is God.
He made us, and we belong to him;
we are his people, we are his flock.

Enter the Temple gates with thanksgiving;
go into his courts with praise.
Give thanks to him and praise him.

The Lord is good;
his love is eternal
and his faithfulness lasts for ever.

Glory to the Father, and to the Son,
    and to the Holy Spirit:
as it was in the beginning, is now,
    and will be for ever. Amen.

Reading   Mark 12:29-31

Jesus said, "The most important [commandment] is this: 'Listen, Israel! The Lord our God is the only Lord. Love the Lord your God with all your heart, with all your soul, with all your mind, and with all your strength.' The second most important commandment is this: 'Love your neighbor as you love yourself.' There is no other commandment more important than these two."

Prayer

Almighty God and Father,
you have brought us to the light of a new day:
keep us safe the whole day through
from every sinful inclination.
May all our thoughts, words and actions
aim at doing what is pleasing in your sight;
through Jesus Christ our Lord.
—Amen.

For the Help of the Saints

May the Blessed Virgin Mary
and all God's holy saints
intercede for us today
that we may be helped and protected
by God whose reign is for ever.
—Amen.

Blessing

May the Lord + order our days and our deeds
in his peace.
—Amen.

A Brief Night Prayer

Hymn

> As twilight now draws near its close,
> Creator of the world, we pray
> That in your goodness you will be
> Our stronghold till the coming day.
>
> Grant rest without disturbing dreams.
> Let nothing lead us into sin.
> Ward off the evil one's assaults.
> Bless, guard this night we now begin.
>
> O loving Father, hear our prayer,
> Through Christ your only Son our Lord:
> One God, with God the Holy Ghost;
> One King, eternally adored.
> —Amen.

Text: *Te lucis ante terminum*, Latin, sixth century.

Psalm 134   A Call to Praise God

> Come, praise the Lord, all his servants,
> all who serve in his Temple at night.
> Raise your hands in prayer in the Temple,
> and praise the Lord!

May the Lord, who made heaven and earth,
bless you from Zion!

Glory to the Father, and to the Son,
and to the Holy Spirit:
as it was in the beginning, is now,
and will be for ever. Amen.

Reading   1 John 4:16

God is love and those who live in love live in union
with God and God lives in union with them.

Prayer

Visit this house, O Lord, we pray,
and drive from it all the snares of the enemy.
May your holy angels dwell here
to keep us in peace and tranquillity,
and may your blessing be always upon us.
We ask this through Christ our Lord.
—Amen.

Final Prayer to Mary

We turn to you for protection,
    holy Mother of God.
Listen to our prayers
    And help us in our needs.

Save us from every danger,
    glorious and blessed Virgin.

Blessing

May the Lord + give us a peaceful night
    as day's perfect ending.
—Amen.

Take courage, toil and strive zealously,
for nothing will be lost.
Every prayer you make,
every psalm you sing is recorded;
every alms, every fast is recorded.

St. Cyril of Jerusalem (ca. 315-386)

2. Prayers for All Seasons

Most prayers flicker briefly before the mind's eye and then vanish into darkness. But every age produces some prayers which find their way into print and survive because they touch the hearts of those who call themselves Christians.

Why do these prayers touch our hearts? Some are associated with great saints whose lives validate their words. But this is not the only reason. Whether written by saints long ago or by men and women of our day, some prayers echo universal desires and sentiments.

Here, then, are prayers for all ages and all seasons.

Prayers From the Heart

Day by Day

Thank you, Lord Jesus Christ,

For all the benefits and blessings which you have
given me,

For all the pains and insults which you have borne
for me.

Merciful Friend, Brother and Redeemer,

May I know you more clearly,

Love you more dearly,

And follow you more nearly,

Day by day.

St. Richard of Chichester (1197-1253)

God Be in My Head

God be in my head and in my understanding.

God be in my eyes and in my looking.

God be in my mouth and in my speaking.

God be in my heart and in my thinking.

God be at my end and my departing.

Sarum Primer (1527)

Saint Patrick's Breastplate

Christ, be with me, Christ before me,
Christ behind me,
Christ in me, Christ beneath me, Christ above me,
Christ on my right, Christ on my left,
Christ where I lie, Christ where I sit, Christ
where I arise,
Christ in the heart of every one who thinks of me,
Christ in the mouth of every one who speaks of me,
Christ in every eye that sees me,
Christ in every ear that hears me.
Salvation is of the Lord.
Salvation is of the Lord,
Salvation is of the Christ.
May your salvation, O Lord, be ever with us.

**Attributed to St. Patrick, the Apostle of
Ireland (ca. 389-461)**

Self-Dedication

Lord, I freely yield all my freedom to you.
Take my memory, my intellect, and my entire will.
You have given me everything I am or have;
I give it all back to you to stand under your
will alone.
Your love and your grace are enough for me;
I shall ask for nothing more.

St. Ignatius Loyola (ca. 1491-1556)

For Perfect Love

My God, I desire to love you perfectly,
With all my heart, which you made for yourself,
With all my mind, which you alone can satisfy,
With all my soul, which longs to soar to you,
With all my strength, my feeble strength
which shrinks from so great a task
and yet can choose nothing else
but spend itself in loving you.
Claim my heart; free my mind;
Uplift my soul; reinforce my strength;
That where I fail, you may succeed in me
and make me love you perfectly,
through Jesus Christ, my Lord.

**Community of St. Mary the Virgin,
Wantage, UK**

For a Magnanimous Heart

Keep us, O God, from all pettiness,
Let us be large in thought, in word, in deed.
Let us be done with fault-finding
and leave off all self-seeking.
May we put away all pretense and meet each other
        face to face,
without self-pity and without prejudice.
May we never be hasty in judgment,

and always generous.
Let us always take time for all things,
and make us grow calm, serene and gentle.
Teach us to put into action our better impulses,
to be straightforward and unafraid.
Grant that we may realize
that it is the little things of life that
        create differences,
that in the big things of life
we are as one.
And, O Lord God, let us not forget to be kind!

Queen Mary Stuart (1542-1587)

For a Holy Heart

Lord, grant me a holy heart
that sees always what is fine and pure
and is not frightened at the sight of sin,
but creates order wherever it goes.
Grant me a heart that knows nothing
of boredom, weeping and sighing.
Let me not be too concerned
with the bothersome thing
I call "myself."
Lord, give me a sense of humor
and I will find happiness in life
and profit for others.

St. Thomas More (1478-1535)

Canticle of Brother Sun and Sister Moon

Most high, almighty, good Lord!
All praise, glory, honor and exaltation are yours!
To you alone do they belong,
and no mere mortal dares pronounce your Name.

Praise to you, O Lord our God, for all your creatures:
first, for our dear Brother Sun,
who gives us the day
and illumines us with his light;
fair is he, in splendor radiant,
bearing your very likeness, O Lord.

For our Sister Moon,
and for the bright, shining stars:
We praise you, O Lord.

For our Brother Wind,
for fair and stormy seasons
and all heaven's varied moods,
by which you nourish all that you have made:
We praise you, O Lord.

For our Sister Water,
so useful, lowly, precious and pure:
We praise you, O Lord.

For our Brother Fire,
who brightens up our darkest nights:
beautiful is he and eager,
invincible and keen:
We praise you, O Lord.

For our Mother Earth,
who sustains and feeds us,
producing fair fruits, many-colored flowers
          and herbs:
We praise you, O Lord.

For those who forgive one another for love of you,
and who patiently bear sickness and other trials.
Happy are they who peacefully endure;
you will crown them, O Most High!
We praise you, O Lord.

For our Sister Death,
the inescapable fact of life
—Woe to those who die in mortal sin!
Happy those she finds doing your will!
From the Second Death they stand immune:
We praise you, O Lord.

All creatures,
praise and glorify my Lord

and give him thanks
and serve him in great humility.
We praise you, O Lord.

St. Francis of Assisi (1181-1226)

Prayers for Light

A Spirit to Know You

Gracious and holy Father,
please give me:
intellect to understand you,
reason to discern you,
diligence to seek you,
wisdom to find you,
a spirit to know you,
a heart to meditate upon you,
ears to hear you,
eyes to see you,
a tongue to proclaim you,
a way of life pleasing to you,
patience to wait for you,
and perseverance to look for you.
Grant me a perfect end—

your holy presence,
a blessed resurrection,
and life everlasting.

Attributed to St. Benedict of Nursia
(ca. 480-555)

For Insight

May the Lord Jesus touch our eyes,
as he did those of the blind.
Then we shall begin to see
in visible things those which are invisible.
May he open our eyes to gaze,
not on present realities,
but on the blessings to come.
May he open the eyes of our heart
to contemplate God in Spirit,
through Jesus Christ the Lord,
to whom belong power and glory through all eternity.

Origen of Alexandria (185-253)

The Road Ahead

My Lord God,
I have no idea where I am going.
I do not see the road ahead of me.
I cannot know for certain where it will end.
Nor do I really know myself,

and the fact that I think that I am following your will
does not mean that I am actually doing so.
But I believe that the desire to please you
does in fact please you.
And I hope I have that desire in all that I am doing.
I hope that I will never do anything apart from
      that desire.
And I know that if I do this,
you will lead me by the right road
though I may know nothing about it.
Therefore will I trust you always
though I may seem to be lost and in the shadow
      of death.
I will not fear, for you are ever with me,
and you will never leave me to face my perils alone.

Thomas Merton (1915-1968)

Flood the Path With Light

God of our life,
there are days when the burdens we carry
chafe our shoulders and weigh us down;
when the road seems dreary and endless,
the skies grey and threatening;
when our lives have no music in them,
and our hearts are lonely,
and our souls have lost their courage.
Flood the path with light,

turn our eyes to where the skies are full of promise;
tune our hearts to brave music;
give us the sense of comradeship
with heroes and saints of every age;
and so quicken our spirits
that we may be able to encourage
the souls of all who journey with us on the
        road of life,
to your honor and glory.

Attributed to St. Augustine of Hippo
(354-430)

For a Good Choice

Dear Father,
you are the creative origin of all I am
and of all I am called to be.
With the talents and opportunities I have,
how may I serve you best?
Please guide my mind and heart,
open me to the needs of my country and
        of the world,
and help me to choose wisely and practically
for your honor and glory
and for the good of all those whose lives I touch.

Make Your Light Shine

God our Father, you who said,
"Let there be light shining out of darkness,"
make your light shine in our hearts
so that the knowledge of the glory of God
which is on the face of Christ
may shine there also.
Throughout this day
may your mercy be our defense;
your praise, our gladness;
your Word, the treasure of our hearts.
Let your blessing descend on each of our actions.
Let it accompany us and help us reach that
      great morning
which knows no night,
when we will praise your love unceasingly,
through your Son Jesus Christ, our Savior
      and brother,
in the unity of the love of the Holy Spirit,
forever and ever.

Lucien Deiss, C.S.Sp.

Truth and Beauty

God our Father,
by the work of your Spirit, living in our hearts,
you lead us to desire your perfection,
to seek for truth and to rejoice in beauty.
Enlighten and inspire
all thinkers, writers, artists and craftsmen,
so that in all things which are true and pure
and beautiful,
your name may be made holy
and your kingdom come on earth.
We ask this through your Son, Jesus Christ our Lord.
Amen.

**St. Anselm's Chapel, Christ Church
Cathedral, Canterbury**

Prayers for Families

For Families

O God our Father,
bind together in your all-embracing love
every family on earth.
Banish anger and bitterness within them;
nourish forgiveness and peace.
Bestow upon parents such wisdom and patience

that they may gently exercise the disciplines of love,
and call forth from their children
their greatest virtue and their highest skill.
Instill in children such independence
          and self-respect
that they may freely obey their parents,
and grow in the joys of companionship.
Open ears to hear the truth
within the words another speaks;
open eyes to see the reality
beneath another's appearance;
and make the mutual affection of families
a sign of your kingdom;
through Jesus Christ our Lord. Amen.

From an Anglican Prayer Book

For Our Family

Father,
from whom all parenthood derives its meaning,
you created men and women
and blessed their union in marriage,
making them a help and support for each other.
Remember our family today,
help us to love one another unselfishly,
as Christ does his Church,
so that we may live together in joy and peace
and give you heartfelt praise,
through your Son and in the Holy Spirit. Amen.

For Our Household

O God of goodness and mercy,
to your fatherly protection we commend
our family,
our household,
and all that belongs to us.
We commit all to your love and keeping.
Fill this house with your blessings,
even as you filled the house of Nazareth
with your presence.

For Family Peace

Holy Father,
if any of us has any grievance against another,
may the sun not set on our anger or disappointment,
but may we present as our offering to you a forgiving heart.
Grant each of us the courage
to forgive those who have offended us,
the patience to bear with our own faults,
and the faith to renew our commitment to you
each day of the year.

Kevin Fleming

For Those We Love

Lord God,
we can hope for others nothing better
than the happiness we desire for ourselves.

Therefore, I pray you,
do not separate me after death
from those I have tenderly loved on earth.
Grant that where I am they may be with me,
and that I may enjoy their presence in heaven
after being so often deprived of it on earth.
Lord God, I ask you to receive your beloved children
immediately into your life-giving heart.
After this brief life on earth,
give them eternal happiness.

St. Ambrose of Milan (334-397)

A Prayer for Husbands and Wives

Father, you called us to found this family together.
Give us the grace to animate it with your love;
May our family always comfort those who live in it
and welcome those who enter it.
Through Christ our Lord. Amen.

The Pope's Family Prayer Book

For Our Children

Lord, help our children
to know the road you have chosen for them:
may they give you glory and attain salvation.
Sustain them with your strength,
and let them not be satisfied with easy goals.

Enlighten us, their parents,
that we may help them to recognize their
     calling in life
and respond to it generously.
May we put no obstacle in the way of your
     inner guidance.

The Pope's Family Prayer Book

I Place Them in Your Care

Lord Jesus Christ,
I praise and thank you
for my parents and my brothers and sisters
whom you have given me to cherish.
Surround them with your tender, loving care,
teach them to love and serve one another in
     true affection
and to look to you in all their needs.
I place them all in your care,
knowing that your love for them is greater than
     my own.
Keep us close to one another in this life
and conduct us at the last to our true and
     heavenly home.
Blessed be God forever. Amen.

For Parents in Trouble

Lord, you are present everywhere.
We ask your help for those of our parents
who are in trouble.
Where they are at odds with each other,
we pray for a breakthrough and reconciliation.
Where a job has been lost,
grant a new opportunity for useful work.
Where there is sickness,
we pray for healing and strength.
Where there are patterns which make life dull,
we pray for a broken routine
which will allow new possibilities.
O Lord,
some of our parents have trouble.
We ask you to help them,
and to help us to know what to do,
through Jesus Christ your Son.

John W. Vannorsdall

Prayer is the key of morning and the bolt of evening.

Mohandas K. Gandhi, the liberator of India (1869-1948)

Prayers for the Human Family

For Love and Service

Lord, you created us for yourself
and our hearts are restless until they rest in you.
Please show us how to love you
with all our heart and our neighbor as ourself.
Teach us to be practical about loving one another
in you and for you and as you desire.
Show us our immediate neighbor today;
call our attention to the needs of others.
Remind us that you count as done to you
what we do for one another,
and that our turning away from one another
is really turning our backs on you.
Make us know, love and serve you in this life
and be happy for ever in the next,
in union with all our sisters and brothers,
children of a common Father.
To serve you is to reign.

For Service to Others

Make us worthy, Lord,
to serve our fellow human beings
throughout the world
who live and die in poverty and hunger.
Give them through our hands this day
their daily bread,
and by our understanding love,
give peace and joy.

Mother Teresa of Calcutta (d. 1998)

For Human Friendship

Father,
you have made us.
Red, yellow, brown, white and black,
tall and short, fat and thin,
rich and poor, young and old—
all are your children.
Teach us to cooperate rather than to compete,
to respect rather than to revile,
to forgive rather than condemn.
Your Son turned from no one.
May we learn, like him,
to be open to the share of the divine
that you have implanted in each of your
        sons and daughters.

And may we forge a bond of love
that will make a living reality the community
      of friendship
in which we profess to believe.

Christopher Prayers for Today

For the Needy

Grant, Lord, that I may gladly share
what I have with the needy,
humbly ask for what I need from those who have,
sincerely admit the evil I have done,
calmly bear the evil I suffer,
not envy my neighbors for their blessings,
and thank you unceasingly
whenever you hear my prayer.

St. Thomas Aquinas, O.P. (1225-1274)

Let Us Not Be Blinded

O Lord,
do not let us turn into "broken cisterns"
that can hold no water. . . .
Do not let us be so blinded
by the enjoyment of the good things of earth
that our hearts become insensible
to the cry of the poor, of the sick,
of orphaned children,
and of those innumerable brothers and sisters of ours

who lack the necessary minimum to eat,
to clothe their nakedness,
and to gather their family together under one roof.

Pope John XXIII (1881-1963)

A Night Prayer for Those in Need

O God, before I sleep,
I remember before you all the people I love,
and now in the silence I say their names to you. . . .
All the people who are sad and lonely,
old and forgotten,
poor and hungry and cold,
in pain of body and in distress of mind.
Bless all who specially need your blessing,
and bless me, too,
and make this a good night for me.
This I ask for your love's sake. Amen.

William Barclay (1907-1978)

For God's Good Earth

Father, the Bible tells us
you looked on all that you made
and saw that it was good.
But we have been too willing
to squander the richness of creation.
We have laid the ax to the mighty forests,
despoiled the green hillsides,

wasted earth's mineral wealth.
We have fouled the air,
littered the countryside,
and polluted the streams and oceans.
Voices are raised to stop us from squandering
      our patrimony.
May we heed them in time
so that one day we can look on the planet
you have given us
and say with pride, once again, "Behold, it is good."

Christopher Prayers for Today

For People of All Ages
Let us pray for our children:
Help them to grow in grace and wisdom,
and in the knowledge of your Son Jesus Christ.
Let us pray for our young men and women:
Give them a full and happy youth;
open their hearts to accept not only the suffering,
but also the joy of the world.
Let us pray for all married people
who have promised before Christ to be faithful to
    each other:
May the fervor of their love show to the world
the tenderness of Christ Jesus toward his Church.
Let us pray for all those in the autumn of life:

Grant them a peaceful and happy old age;
guide their steps on the road to peace.
Let us pray for all those who have no family and
    home:
Show the gentleness of your presence
to all who live alone
and have no hope but you.

Lucien Deiss, C.S.Sp.

Prayers for Justice and Peace

Prayer of St. Francis

Lord, make me an instrument of your peace:
where there is hatred, let me sow love;
where there is injury, pardon;
where there is doubt, faith;
where there is despair, hope;
where there is darkness, light;
and where there is sadness, joy.
O Divine Master,
grant that I may not so much seek
to be consoled as to console,
to be understood as to understand,
to be loved as to love.
For it is in giving that we receive,
it is in pardoning that we are pardoned,
and it is in dying that we are born to eternal life.

Attributed to St. Francis of Assisi (1181-1226)

Prayer for Peace

Most holy God,
The source of all good desires,
All right judgements, and all just works:
Give to us your servants, that peace which the world
      cannot give,
So that our minds may be fixed on the doing of
      your will,
And that we, being delivered from the fear of
      all enemies,
May live in peace and quietness;
Through the mercies of Christ Jesus our Savior.
Amen.

Book of Common Prayer, 1979

For Reconciliation

Lord God,
out of your great love for the world,
you reconciled earth to heaven
through your only-begotten Son, our Savior.
In the darkness of our sins,
we fail to love one another as we should;
please pour your light into our souls
and fill us with your tenderness
that we may embrace our friends in you
and our enemies for your sake,

in a bond of mutual affection.
We make our prayer through the same
Christ our Lord. Amen.

Visigothic Liturgy

Prayer for Concord

God the Father,
origin of all that is divine,
good beyond all that is good,
fair beyond all that is fair,
in you is calmness, peace, and concord.
Heal what divides us from one another
and bring us back into the unity of love,
bearing some likeness to your divine nature.
Through the embrace of love
and the bonds of godly affection,
make us one in the Spirit
by that peace of yours
that makes all things peaceful.
We ask this through the grace, mercy, and tenderness
of your only begotten Son, Jesus Christ our Lord.
Amen.

St. Dionysius of Alexandria (+264)

For Our Nation

Eternal God,
have mercy on the faithful
for whom our Lord and Savior Jesus Christ
poured out his precious blood.
Through your only-begotten Son
avert the dangers
which threaten our people and country.

St. Peter Canisius, S.J. (1521-1597)

For Civil Authorities

Almighty and ever-living God,
in whose hand are the rights and hopes of
  every people,
look graciously on those who govern,
that in lasting peace they may promote
social progress and religious freedom
for all the nations of the earth.
Through Christ our Lord. Amen.

The Pope's Family Prayer Book

A Prayer for Peacemakers

O Lord, God of peace,
you have created us and shown us your love
so that we may share in your glory.
We bless you and give thanks
because you have sent us Jesus, your
        well-beloved Son.
Through the mystery of his resurrection,
you made him the worker of salvation,
the source of peace, the bond of brotherhood.
We give thanks for the desires, efforts,
        and achievements
stirred up by the Spirit of peace in our time,
to replace hate by love,
mistrust by understanding,
indifference by interdependence.
Open our minds and hearts to the real demands
        of love,
so that we may become more completely
        peacemakers.
Remember, Father of mercy,
all who struggle, suffer, and die
to bring forth a world of closer relationship.
May your kingdom of justice, peace, and love
come to people of every race and tongue.
May the earth be filled with your glory.

Pope Paul VI (1897-1978)

Peace in Our Days

Almighty and eternal God,
may your grace enkindle in all
a love for the many unfortunate people
whom poverty and misery reduce to a condition
        of life
unworthy of human beings.
Arouse in the hearts of those who call you Father
a hunger and thirst for justice and peace,
and for fraternal charity in deeds and in truth.
Grant, O Lord,
peace in our days,
peace to souls,
peace to families,
peace to our country,
and peace among nations.

Pope Pius XII (1876-1958)

Prayers for the Church

For the Church

Gracious Father,
we pray to you for your holy Catholic Church.
Fill it with your truth.

Keep it in your peace.
Where it is corrupt, reform it.
Where it is in error, correct it.
Where it is right, defend it.
Where it is in want, provide for it.
Where it is divided, reunite it;
for the sake of your Son, our Savior Jesus Christ.

**William Laud, Archbishop of
Canterbury (1573-1645)**

For the Church of Your Son Jesus

God our Father, we pray to you
for the Church of your Son Jesus.
Let her be resplendent with the beauty of Jesus;
let her avoid painting herself with the vain beauty
        of the world.
Let her not be disfigured by the wrinkles of old age;
let her represent for all people the hope of
        the future.
Let her face be purified from every stain of pride;
let her show preference for the poor and the humble.
Let her be holy and spotless;
let her not be maimed by error.
Let her be beautiful as one betrothed,
all dressed up for her spouse;
let her shun the unseemly "adornments"
of money and power.

Lord Jesus, you have loved your Church,
and you have given yourself up for her;
we pray to you:
Guide this Church that she, in turn,
will love all people,
and put herself at their service.

Lucien Deiss, C.S.Sp.

For the Pope

Almighty Father in heaven,
shelter under your protective care
our holy father, Pope *Name.*
Direct him according to your loving kindness
in the way of eternal salvation for all of us.
Lord Jesus, the one true shepherd,
guide the Pope in the care of your people on earth.
Through the Holy Spirit
which you have given him
be his light, his strength, and his consolation.
Through your help
may he ever teach the truth
and accomplish always what is pleasing to you,
O Holy Trinity!

For Our Bishop

O God, you sent the Lord Jesus
for the good of the whole world.

Through him you chose the apostles,
and after them, from one generation to another,
you have ordained for us saintly bishops.
God of truth, fill our bishop, *Name*, with life,
and make him a worthy successor of the apostles.
Give him grace and the power of the Holy Spirit,
the Spirit you gave so generously to your servants,
the prophets and patriarchs.
Make him a worthy shepherd of your flock,
living as our bishop,
blamelessly and without offense.

Bishop Serapion's Prayer Book (4th century)

The Good Shepherd

Gather together your sheep, Lord,
in all the places where they have been scattered
during the mist and darkness.
Lead them to good pasturage,
let them rest in good grazing ground.
Those who are lost—search out;
those who have strayed—bring back.
Those who are wounded—bind their wounds;
those who are sick—cure.
Those bearing young—watch over them;
all of your sheep—keep them safe in your flock.

Lord Jesus,
because you are our good shepherd,
help us all to be the sheep of your flock.
Gather all into the fold of your love
so that there may be but one flock
and only one shepherd.

Lucien Deiss, C.S.Sp.

Prayer for Vocations

God our Father,
you will all to be saved
and come to the knowledge of the truth.
Send workers into your harvest
that the gospel may be preached to every creature
and your people,
gathered together by the word of life
and strengthened by the power of the sacraments,
may advance in the way of salvation and love.
Please grant this through Christ our Lord. Amen.

Prayers for Strength

Like Children

Like children playing on the beach
we have built houses of sand.
The wave of time has come

and the laughter of the tides has submerged
        everything.
But we know, Lord,
that if our earthly home is destroyed
you will build us an eternal home near you
        in heaven.
Give us strength to leave our earthly dwellings
and our games in the sand.
Direct our boat toward the shores of eternity.

Lucien Deiss, C.S.Sp.

For Courage

Lord Jesus, teach me to be generous;
teach me to serve you as you deserve,
to give and not to count the cost,
to fight and not to heed the wounds,
to toil and not to seek for rest,
to labor and not to seek reward,
except that of knowing that I do your will.

St. Ignatius Loyola (1491-1556)

Into Your Hands

Father,
I abandon myself into your hands;
do with me what you will.
Whatever you may do, I thank you:
I am ready for all, I accept all.

Let only your will be done in me,
and in all your creatures—
I wish no more than this, O Lord.
Into your hands I commend my soul;
I offer it to you with all the love of my heart,
for I love you, Lord,
and so need to give myself,
to surrender myself into your hands without reserve,
and with boundless confidence,
for you are my Father.

Charles de Foucauld (1858-1916)

Light Up the Small Duties
O Father,
light up the small duties of this day's life:
may they shine with the beauty of
        your countenance.
May we believe that glory can dwell
in the commonest task of every day.

St. Augustine of Hippo (354-430)

For Perseverance
O Lord,
keep us from the vain strife of words
and help us profess the truth.
Preserve us in the faith,

true faith and undefiled,
that we may always hold fast what we promised
when we were baptized
in the Name of the Father, the Son, and the Holy Spirit.
May we have you for our Father,
and may we always live in your Son
and in the fellowship of the Holy Spirit,
through the same Christ Jesus our Lord. Amen.

St. Hilary of Poitiers (+368)

Now Let Me Accept

O heavenly Father,
I praise and thank you for the peace of the night;
I praise and thank you for this new day;
I praise and thank you for all your goodness
and faithfulness throughout my life.
You have granted me many blessings.
Now let me also accept what is hard from your hand.
You will lay on me no more than I can bear.
You make all things work together
for the good of your children.

Dietrich Bonhoeffer,
pastor and martyr (1906-1945)

A Prayer to the Holy Cross

By you hell is despoiled, O Holy Cross.
By you its mouth is stopped up to all the redeemed.

By you demons are made afraid and restrained,
    conquered and trampled under foot.
By you the world is renewed
    and made beautiful with truth,
    governed by the light of righteousness.
By you sinful humanity is justified,
    the condemned are saved,
    the servants of sin and hell are set free,
    the dead are raised to life.
By you the blessed city in heaven is restored
    and made perfect.
By you God, the Son of God willed for our sakes
    "to become obedient to the Father, even
        unto death,"
Because of which he is exalted and has received
    "the Name which is above every other name."
By you "his throne is prepared"
    and his kingdom established.

St. Anselm of Canterbury (1033-1109)

Prayer to Michael the Archangel

Holy Michael the Archangel,
defend us in battle.
Be our protection against the wickedness
and snares of the devil.
May God rebuke him, we humbly pray,

And do thou, O Prince of the heavenly host,
by the power of God,
thrust into hell Satan and all wicked spirits
who wander through the world for the ruin of souls.

Pope Leo XIII (1878-1903)

Prayers in Time of Illness

Raise Me Up, Lord

Raise me up, Lord,
do not abandon your servant.
I want health that I may sing to you
and help your people lead holy lives.
I plead with you:
you are my strength, do not desert me.
I have grown weak amid the storm
but I long to return to you.

St. Gregory of Nazianzus (329-389)

Lord Jesus, Healer

Lord Jesus, healer of our souls and bodies,
during your life on earth,
you went about doing good,
healing every manner of sickness and disease,
strengthening, curing, comforting and consoling.

You want nothing more
than to see us healthy and happy.
You are the enemy of death and disease,
and in and through you
they are overcome and conquered.
Lay your healing hands upon us now,
so that we may live in your praise untiringly.

For Recovery From Sickness

God of heavenly power,
one word from you can free us
from every weakness and disease.
Kindly hear our prayers,
free us from our sickness,
restore our health,
and give us the vigor to praise you unceasingly.
We ask this through Christ our Lord. Amen.

Gallican Liturgy (7th century)

For the Sick

Father, your only Son took upon himself
the sufferings and weakness of the whole
human race;
through his passion and cross
he taught us how good can be brought out of
suffering.

Look upon our brothers and sisters who are ill.
In the midst of illness and pain,
may they be united with Christ,
who heals both body and soul;
may they know the consolation
promised to those who suffer
and be fully restored to health.
Through Christ our Lord. Amen.

The Pope's Family Prayer Book

In Time of Sickness

Lord Jesus,
you suffered and died for me;
you understand suffering
and you share it with us.
Teach me to accept my pains,
to bear them in union with you,
and to offer them up
for the forgiveness of my sins
and for the welfare of the living and the dead.
Calm my fears, increase my trust in you;
make me patient and cooperative
with those who serve me,
and if it be your will,
please restore me to health,
so that I may work for your honor and glory
and for the salvation of all.

In Time of Serious Illness

God, Our Father, Eternal Mystery,
I believe in your boundless, unchanging love.
You have created me for yourself,
to enjoy your peace and love for all eternity.
Help me to overcome my failings,
my fear of suffering,
my dread of the unknown.
I will do all in my power to improve or regain
my health,
and fulfill all the obligations of my state in life,
particularly to those nearest me.
Bring me finally to perfect union with your will.
I accept now the time, place, and manner of
my death,
knowing it is but a change to an infinitely better life
with you.
Yes, Lord, I want to serve you.
Yes, I want to be with you.

Robert L. Mutchler

Your Will Be Done

God and loving Father,
your will be done.
I offer my sickness with all its suffering to you,
together with all that my Savior has suffered for me.

73

By the power of his blessed passion,
have mercy on me
and free me from this illness and pain
if it be according to your will and for my good.
Lord, I entrust my life and my death to you;
do with me as you please.
In sickness and in health,
I only want to love you always.

Prayer to Mary for the Sick

Mary, health of the sick,
Be at the bedside of all the world's sick people;
of those who are unconscious and dying;
of those who have begun their agony;
of those who have abandoned all hope of a cure;
of those who weep and cry out in pain:
of those who cannot receive care
because they have no money;
of those who ought to be resting
but are forced by poverty to work;
of those who seek vainly in their beds
for a less painful position;
of those who pass long nights sleepless;
of those who are tormented
by the cares of a family in distress;
of those who must renounce
their most cherished plans for the future;
of those, above all, who do not believe in a better life;

of those who rebel and curse God;
of those who do not know that Christ
suffered like them and for them.

Rabboni

Prayers for the Journey

You Are Waiting to Surprise Us
God our Father,
you are waiting in the future
to surprise us with love.
Help us to welcome you with joy
whenever you appear,
so that we may live like excited children,
always expecting you.
Through Jesus Christ our Lord. Amen.

Let My Soul Take Refuge
O God, full of compassion,
I commit and commend myself to you,
in whom I am, and live, and know.
Be the goal of my pilgrimage,
and my rest by the way.
Let my soul take refuge from the crowding turmoil

of worldly thought beneath the shadow of
      your wings;
Let my heart, this sea of restless waves,
find peace in you, O God.

St. Augustine of Hippo (354-430)

Now That I Have Found You

Like a thirsty child reaching for a drink,
I grasp for you, O God.
And I have found you.
I have sensed your holy presence in the
      worship service;
And in the hour of prayer I have felt you to be near.
I realize now that your love for me
is far better than life itself.
My heart is full of joy and contentment.
My mouth is filled with praises for you.
Even the night hours are no longer lonely
As I contemplate your tender concern for me.
The enemies of my soul still seek to betray me,
But they shall not snatch me out of your hand.
And now that I have found you,
I shall be secure and happy forever.

Leslie F. Brandt (Paraphrase of Psalm 63)

God of Our Childhood

God of our childhood,
you whose name we have learned
in the smiles of our father and mother,
we beg you:
Preserve in us a childlike spirit
so that we can enter your Kingdom.
God of our adolescence,
you who have created the eagerness of youth,
who know its desires and its follies,
we beg you:
Preserve the flower of hope in our hearts,
be always the God of the joy of our youth.
God of our maturity,
you who call each person
to make fruitful the gifts you have put in him,
we beg you:
Help each of us to become that perfect person
who realizes the fullness of Christ.
God of our old age,
at the time when the spirit loses its ardor,
when the body becomes feeble,
we beg you:
Remain close to us when the night comes.
You are our God for all eternity.

Lucien Deiss, C.S.Sp.

"Fear Not, for I Have Redeemed You"

Thus says the Lord:
He who created you, O Jacob,
He who formed you, O Israel:
"Fear not, for I have redeemed you;
I have called you by name and you are mine.
When you pass through the waters
    I will be with you
and through the rivers,
    they shall not overwhelm you;
when you walk through fire
    you shall not be burned,
    and the flame shall not consume you.
For I am the Lord your God,
the Holy One of Israel, your Savior.
And you are precious in my eyes,
    and cherished,
    and I love you."

Isaiah 43:1-4 (NRSV)

I Have Spent My Life, Lord

I have spent my life, Lord,
tuning up my lyre
instead of singing to you.
    I'm sorry, Lord.

I have spent my life, Lord,
looking for my own path

instead of walking with you.
    I'm sorry, Lord.

I have spent my life, Lord,
begging for love
instead of loving you in my brothers and sisters.
    I'm sorry, Lord.

I have spent my life, Lord,
fleeing the night instead of saying:
You are my light.
    I'm sorry, Lord.

I have spent my life, Lord,
seeking security
instead of placing my hand in yours.
    I'm sorry, Lord.

I have spent my life, Lord,
making resolutions and not keeping them.
    I'm sorry, Lord.

Now, if it is true, Lord,
that you save us
not because of our works
but because of your great mercy,
then we are now ready
to receive your salvation.

Lucien Deiss, C.S.Sp.

Prayers Near Journey's End

For the Aged
Eternal Father,
unchanged down the changing years,
be near to those who are aged.
Even though their bodies weaken,
grant that their spirit may be strong.
May they bear weariness and affliction with patience,
and at the end, meet death with serenity.
Through Christ our Lord. Amen.

The Pope's Family Prayer Book

For the Dying
Lord,
this night some will be gathered to the Father.
Grant that they may go forth
surrounded by their loved ones,
without pain of body,
with clarity of mind,
and joyful expectancy of soul.

J. M. Ford

*Do what you can and then pray that God will
give you the power to do what you cannot.*

St. Augustine of Hippo (354-430)

Stay With Us, Lord

Stay with us, Lord:
Behold, evening is coming,
and we still haven't recognized your face
in each of our brothers and sisters.
Stay with us, Lord Jesus Christ!

Stay with us, Lord:
Behold, evening is coming,
and we still haven't shared your bread
in thanksgiving with all our brothers and sisters.
Stay with us, Lord Jesus Christ!

Stay with us, Lord:
behold, evening is coming,
and we still haven't recognized your Word
in the words of all our brothers and sisters.
Stay with us, Lord Jesus Christ!

Stay with us, Lord:
behold, evening is coming,
and our hearts are still too slow to believe
that you had to die in order to rise again.
Stay with us, Lord Jesus Christ!

Stay with us, Lord,
for our night itself becomes day

when you are there!
Stay with us, Lord Jesus Christ!

Lucien Deiss, C.S.Sp.

Prayer for a Happy Death
Lord Jesus Christ,
you want everyone's salvation
and no one ever appeals to you in vain,
for with your own lips you promised:
"Whatever you ask the Father in my name, I will do."
In your name—Jesus, Savior—
I ask that in my dying moments
you will give me full use of my senses,
heart-felt sorrow for my sins,
firm faith, hope in good measure, and perfect love,
that I may be able to say honestly to you:
"Into your hands, O Lord, I commend my spirit.
You have redeemed me, Lord God of truth."

St. Vincent Ferrer (1350-1419)

Come to Me Like a Cry of Joy
When my life sinks in sadness,
come to me like a cry of joy.
Come, Lord Jesus Christ!

When my heart is as hard as a rock,
come to me like the dew of springtime.
Come, Lord Jesus Christ!

When noise invades my haven,
come to me like an oasis of silence.
Come, Lord Jesus Christ!

When the wind of hate rises within me,
come to me like a kiss of pardon.
Come, Lord Jesus Christ!

When I am sinking into the darkness of death,
come to me like a child's smile.
Come, Lord Jesus Christ!

And when the earth encloses me in its arms,
open for me the doors of your mercy.
Come, Lord Jesus Christ!

Lucien Deiss, C.S.Sp.

For the Gift of Final Perseverance

I pray you, noble Jesus,
that as you have graciously granted me
joyfully to imbibe the words of your knowledge,
so you will also of your bounty
grant me to come at length to you,

the fount of all wisdom,
and to dwell in your presence for ever.

St. Bede the Venerable (673-735)

For the Faithful Departed

By the merits of your rising from the dead,
Lord Christ,
let death no longer have dominion
over the faithful departed.
Grant to your servants
a resting place in your eternal mansions
and in the arms of Abraham and Sarah,
our ancestors in the faith.
Grant this to all who,
from Adam and Eve to this day,
have served you with a clean heart—
to our mothers and fathers,
to our sisters and brothers,
to our friends and kindred.
Make a place in your heavenly kingdom, Lord,
for everyone who has done you faithful service
in this present life
and to all who, in their fashion,
have striven toward you.

An Ancient Prayer

For Those Who Have Gone Before Us

Antiphon:
The Lord will open to them the gates of paradise,
and they will return to that homeland
where there is no death, but only lasting joy.

Give them eternal rest, O Lord,
—And let them share your glory.

Prayer
O God, our Creator and Redeemer,
by your power Christ conquered death
and returned to you in glory.
May all your people
who have gone before us in faith
share his victory
and enjoy the vision of your glory for ever,
where Christ lives and reigns with you and the
        Holy Spirit,
one God, for ever and ever.
—Amen.

Roman Missal

And Peace at Last

May he support us all the day long,
till the shadows lengthen
and the evening comes
and the busy world is hushed
and the fever of life is over
and our work is done
—then in his mercy—
may he give us a safe lodging
and a holy rest
and peace at the last.

Attributed to John Henry Newman (1801-1890)

*The Christian ideal has not been tried and
found wanting.
It has been found difficult and left untried.*

G. K. Chesterton (1874-1936)

3. The Week With Christ

Sunday	The Blessed Trinity
Monday	The Holy Spirit
Tuesday	All Saints
	All Souls
Wednesday	St. Joseph
Thursday	The Blessed Sacrament
Friday	The Sacred Heart of Jesus
Saturday	The Blessed Virgin Mary

Days of the Lord

From the very beginning of their existence as a people, Christians have dedicated days of the week to the several mysteries of their redemption, so that by meditating on them one by one they might enter more and more deeply into their meaning and their saving power.

In recent centuries the dedications used here have become widespread among Catholics.

On the *Lord's Day* we commemorate the Blessed Trinity: God as a family of co-equal persons, the sum total of all the mysteries of faith. The many incidents and layers of meaning to be found in the Lord's Day—Easter, Pentecost, Parousia—are fulfilled in the worship of the Triune God who is ever active on our behalf. YHWH is the Name of our God: God-for-us, God-with-us, God-on-our-side.

On *Monday* we concentrate upon the work of the Holy Spirit, the active presence of God in our hearts and in our Christian families and communities. The Holy Spirit pours forth the love of God in our hearts, inspires us to perpetual prayer, and guides us into all truth, as Jesus promised. Come, Holy Spirit!

On *Tuesday* we commemorate all who have fallen asleep in Christ, either those who have achieved the fullness of faith and devotion (the saints) or those who still need our prayers in the communion of saints (the souls in purgatory). The fellowship of faith knows no boundaries of time and space.

On *Wednesday* we pause to honor St. Joseph, the husband of Mary, the foster-father of Jesus, the humble, hard-working carpenter of Nazareth. We see in him complete trust in God, unquestioning obedience, and total dedication to the welfare of others. He is the special patron of those who labor with their hands and of the universal Church.

On *Thursday* our thoughts turn to the Blessed Sacrament, instituted at the Last Supper on Holy Thursday evening. It is the fulfillment of the many sacrifices of the Old Law, the present celebration of the people of the New Covenant, and the anticipation of the final in-gathering when all God's children will sit down at the welcome table of the eternal and heavenly banquet.

On *Friday* we commemorate the suffering of Jesus who freely accepted death for us all and now reigns in glory as the Lord of life. Love is the only explanation for his total self-giving on our behalf. His pierced heart is the guarantee of our salvation: it is the undying source of the saving waters of baptism and of the chalice of salvation from which we all drink. Nothing can separate us from the love of God revealed in Christ!

On *Saturday* we recall Mary's role in our salvation. God-is-with-us (Emmanuel) through the free consent and cooperation of the Blessed Virgin Mary. She treasured all the incidents of the incarnation and "meditated on them in her heart" (Luke 2:19); she stood upright at the foot of the cross, the Mother of Sorrows, Our Lady of Compassion (John 19:25); at Pentecost she was present in the upper room at the birth of the Church (Acts 1:14).

She is the mother of Christ, the mother of the Church, the mother of each believing soul.

Praying in this way—morning and evening—"we shall be spared the possibility of temptation and spiritual ruin, since we remember Christ at all times" (Hippolytus of Rome, *The Apostolic Tradition, 41*).

In group recitation—families, for example—the stanzas of the hymns, psalms, and canticles may be alternated between the leader and the group or the group may divide in two and alternate the stanzas between the two halves. All recite the antiphons before and after the psalms and canticles; the leader initiates the antiphon to the asterisk. Refer to the text for Sunday morning for more indications how to pray together smoothly in groups.

Holy Scripture is the table of Christ, from whence we are nourished, from whence we learn what we should love and what we should desire, to whom we should have our eyes raised.

Alcuin of York (ca. 735-804)

Sunday—The Blessed Trinity

Morning Prayer
Leader: O Lord, + open my lips.
All: And my mouth will proclaim your praise.
Leader: Come, let us worship the true God:
All: One in Three and Three in One.

Hymn
Father most holy, merciful and tender;
Jesus our Savior, with the Father reigning;
Spirit of mercy, Advocate, Defender,
Light never waning.

Trinity sacred, Unity unshaken;
Deity perfect, giving and forgiving,
Light of the angels, Life of the forsaken,
Hope of all living.

Maker of all things, all your creatures praise you;
Lo, all things serve you through your whole creation:
Hear us, Almighty, hear us as we raise you
Hearts adoration.

To the Almighty Triune God be glory:
highest and greatest, help now our endeavor;

we too who praise you, giving honor worthy
now and for ever. Amen.

Text: Tenth-century hymn, trans. P.D. in Elizabeth Goudge, *A Diary of Prayer* (New York: Coward-McCann, Inc., 1966), pp. 95-96.

Psalm 8   God's Glory and Human Dignity

Antiphon   Blessed be the Creator * and Governor
of all things, the Holy and
Undivided Trinity!

O Lord, our Lord,
your greatness is seen in all the world!

Your praise reaches up to the heavens;
it is sung by children and babies.
You are safe and secure from all your enemies;
you stop anyone who opposes you.

When I look at the sky, which you have made,
at the moon and the stars,
which you set in their places—
what are human beings, that you think of them;
mere mortals, that you care for them?

Yet you made them inferior only to yourself;
you crowned them with glory and honor.

You appointed them rulers over everything
        you made;
you placed them over all creation:
sheep and cattle, and the wild animals too;
the birds and the fish
and the creatures of the seas.

O Lord, our Lord,
your greatness is seen in all the world!

Antiphon   Blessed be the Creator and Governor
            of all things, the Holy and Undivided
            Trinity!

Psalm Prayer

Leader: Let us pray (pause for silent prayer)

Blessed Trinity,
as we contemplate your majesty
displayed in the heavens,
help us to honor our human dignity
and to cooperate with you for the good of all;
through Christ Jesus our Lord.
All: Amen.

Reading   Romans 11:33-36

Reader: How great are God's riches! How deep are his wisdom and knowledge! Who can explain his decisions? Who can understand his ways? As the scripture says, "Who knows the mind of the Lord? Who is able to give him advice? Who has ever given him anything, so that he had to pay it back?" For all things were created by him, and all things exist through him and for him. To God be the glory for ever! Amen.

Response

Leader: Let us bless the Father and the Son with the Holy Spirit.
All: Let us praise and glorify God for ever!

Canticle of Zachary   Luke 1:68-79

Antiphon   Holy, holy, holy! * The Lord almighty is holy! His glory fills the whole world.

Blessed be + the Lord, the God of Israel;
    he has come to his people and set them free.

He has raised up for us a mighty Savior,
    born of the house of his servant David.

Through his holy prophets he promised of old
    that he would save us from our enemies,
    and from the hands of all who hate us.

He promised to show mercy to our ancestors
    and to remember his holy covenant.

This was the oath he swore to our father Abraham:
    to set us free from the hands of our enemies,
free to worship him without fear,
    holy and righteous in his sight
    all the days of our life.

You, my child, shall be called the prophet of the
        Most High;
    for you will go before the Lord to prepare his way,
to give his people knowledge of salvation
    by the forgiveness of their sins.

In the tender compassion of our God
    the dawn from on high shall break upon us,
to shine on those who dwell in darkness and the
        shadow of death,
    and to guide our feet into the way of peace.

Glory to the Father, and to the Son
    and to the Holy Spirit:
as it was in the beginning, is now,
    and will be for ever. Amen.

Antiphon   Holy, holy, holy! The Lord almighty is
holy! His glory fills the whole world.

Prayer

Leader: Let us pray (pause for silent prayer)

Father,
you sent your Word to bring us truth
and your Spirit to make us holy.
Through them we come to know the mystery of
        your life.
Help us to worship you, one God in three Persons,
by proclaiming and living our faith in you.
Grant this through our Lord Jesus Christ, your Son,
who lives and reigns with you and the Holy Spirit,
one God, for ever and ever.
All: Amen.

Blessing

Leader: May almighty God,
the Father, + the Son, and the Holy Spirit
bless us and keep us.
All: Amen.

*****

Baptism in the Apostolic Tradition, Rome, ca. 215

The priest who is baptizing asks the candidate standing in the baptismal pool: "Do you believe in God the Father almighty?" The one who is being baptized answers: "I do believe." Then the priest immerses him/her for the first time.

Then he asks the candidate: "Do you believe in Christ Jesus, the Son of God, who was born of the Holy Spirit of the Virgin Mary, and who was crucified under Pontius Pilate, died and rose again on the third day and ascended into heaven and sits at the right hand of the Father and who will come to judge the living and the dead?" When the candidate replies: "I do believe," the priest immerses him/her a second time.

Then he asks the candidate again: "Do you believe in the Holy Spirit, in the Holy Church, in the resurrection of the body?" The candidate replies again: "I do believe," and is immersed a third time.

St. Hippolytus of Rome, bishop and martyr (d. 235)

*****

Evening Prayer

O God, + come to my assistance.
—O Lord, make haste to help me.

Hymn

O radiant Light, O Sun divine
Of God the Father's deathless face,
O Image of the light sublime
That fills the heavenly dwelling place.

O Son of God, the source of life,
Praise is your due by night and day;
Our happy lips must raise the strain
Of your esteemed and splendid name.

Lord Jesus Christ, as daylight fades,
As shine the lights of eventide,
We praise the Father with the Son,
The Spirit blest and with them one.

Text: *Phos hilaron*, Greek, late second century.

Psalm 100   **Praise to the Holy Trinity**

Antiphon   Let us adore the true God, *
One in Three and Three in One.

Sing to the Lord, all the world!
Worship the Lord with joy;
come before him with happy songs!

Acknowledge that the Lord is God.
He made us and we belong to him;
we are his people, we are his flock.

Enter the Temple gates with thanksgiving;
go into his courts with praise.
Give thanks to him and praise him.

The Lord is good;
his love is eternal
and his faithfulness lasts for ever.

Antiphon   Let us adore the true God,
                  One in Three and Three in One.

Psalm Prayer

Almighty and everlasting God,
to you we owe the grace of professing the true faith,
confessing the glory of the eternal Trinity
and adoring its majestic unity.
Confirm us in this faith
and defend us against all adversities.
We ask this through Jesus Christ our Lord,

who lives and reigns with you and the Holy Spirit,
one God, for ever and ever.
—Amen.

Reading   Matthew 28:18-20

Jesus said to his disciples: "I have been given all authority in heaven and on earth. Go, then, to all peoples everywhere and make them my disciples: baptize them in the name of the Father, the Son, and the Holy Spirit, and teach them to obey everything I have commanded you. And I will be with you always, to the end of the age."

Response

Holy, holy, holy Lord, God of power and might.
—Heaven and earth are full of your glory.

Canticle of Mary   Luke 1:46-55

Antiphon   Holy is God, * holy and strong,
             holy and living for ever!

My soul + proclaims the greatness of the Lord,
my spirit rejoices in God my Savior;
for he has looked with favor on his lowly servant.

From this day all generations will call me blessed:
the Almighty has done great things for me,
and holy is his Name.

He has mercy on those who fear him
in every generation.

He has shown the strength of his arm,
he has scattered the proud in their conceit.

He has cast down the mighty from their thrones,
and has lifted up the lowly.

He has filled the hungry with good things,
and the rich he has sent away empty.

He has come to the help of his servant Israel
for he has remembered his promise of mercy,
the promise he made to our ancestors,
to Abraham and his children for ever.

Glory to the Father, and to the Son,
    and to the Holy Spirit:
as it was in the beginning, is now,
    and will be for ever. Amen.

Antiphon   Holy is God, holy and strong,
                holy and living for ever!

Litany of the Holy Trinity (see pp. 286–288) or this prayer

God, we praise you:
Father all-powerful, Christ Lord and Savior,
      Spirit of love.
You reveal yourself in the depths of our being,
drawing us to share in your life and your love.
One God, three Persons,
be near to the people formed in your image,
close to the world your love brings to life.
We ask this, Father, Son, and Holy Spirit,
One God, true and living,
forever and ever.
—Amen.

Blessing

May almighty God,
the Father, + the Son, and the Holy Spirit
bless us and keep us.
—Amen.

Every day at the end of Evening Prayer, the Salve Regina *may be used to conclude this hour; see p. 374.*

Monday—The Holy Spirit

Morning Prayer

O Lord, + open my lips.
—And my mouth will proclaim your praise.
The Spirit of the Lord fills the whole world.
—Come, let us adore our advocate and guide.

Hymn

Holy Spirit, font of light
    focus of God's glory bright,
    shed on us a shining ray.
Father of the fatherless,
    giver of gifts limitless,
    come and touch our hearts today.

Source of strength and sure relief,
    comforter in time of grief,
    enter in and be our guest.
On our journey grant us aid,
    freshening breeze and cooling shade,
    in our labor inward rest.

Enter each aspiring heart,
    occupy its inmost part,
    with your dazzling purity.

All that gives to human worth,
    all that benefits the earth,
    you bring to maturity.

With your soft refreshing rains
    break our drought, remove our stains;
    bind up all our injuries.
Shake with rushing wind our will;
    melt with fire our icy chill;
    bring to light our perjuries.

As your promise we believe
    make us ready to receive
    gifts from your unbounded store.
Grant enabling energy,
    courage in adversity,
    joys that last for evermore.

Text: The Sequence of Pentecost, *Veni, Sancte Spiritus*, attributed to Stephen Langton, Archbishop of Canterbury (d. 1228), trans. John Webster Grant (The Hymn Book of the Anglican Church and the United Church of Canada, Toronto, 1971/1994), #248.

Psalm 104   God, Creator and Provider

Antiphon   Tongues of fire * touched each
person there.

I will bless you, Lord my God!
You fill the world with awe.
You dress yourself in light,
in rich, majestic light.

You stretched the sky like a tent,
built your house beyond the rain.
You ride upon the clouds,
the wind becomes your wings,
the storm becomes your herald,
your servants bolts of light.

You drench the hills
with rain from high heaven.
You nourish the earth
with what your create.

You make grass grow for cattle,
make plants grow for people,
food to eat from the earth
and wine to warm the heart,
oil to glisten on faces
and bread for bodily strength.
God, how fertile your genius!

You shape each thing,
you fill the world
with what you do.

All look to you for food
when they hunger;
you provide it and they feed.
You open your hand, they feast;
you turn away, they fear.

You steal their breath,
they drop back into dust.
Breathe into them, they rise;
the face of the earth comes alive!

Let God's glory endure
and the Lord delight in creating.
I will sing to my God,
make music for the Lord
as long as I live.

Antiphon   Tongues of fire touched each
             person there.

Psalm Prayer

> Creator and Preserver of the universe,
> you continually renew our lives
> by fresh outpourings of the Holy Spirit.
> We thank you for all your gifts
> and look to you for every blessing
> so that we may be perfect in your sight.
> We ask this through Christ our Lord.
> —Amen.

Reading   Acts 2:14-19

> Peter stood up with the other eleven apostles and in a loud voice began to speak to the crowd: "... This is what the prophet Joel spoke about:
>
> 'This is what I will do in the last days, God says:
> I will pour out my Spirit on everyone.
> Your sons and daughters will proclaim my message;
> your young men will see visions,
> and your old men will have dreams.
> Yes, even on my servants, both men and women.
> I will pour out my Spirit in those days,
> and they will proclaim my message.
> I will perform miracles in the sky above
> and wonders on the earth below. . . .
> And then, whoever calls out to the Lord for help will
>   be saved'" (cf. Joel 2:28-32).

Response

The apostles were all filled with the Holy Spirit,
—And began to speak as the Spirit prompted them.

Canticle of Zachary   Luke 1:68-79

Antiphon   Receive the Holy Spirit. *
               When you forgive sins, they are
               forgiven, alleluia!

Blessed be + the Lord, the God of Israel;
     he has come to his people and set them free.

He has raised up for us a mighty Savior,
     born of the house of his servant David.

Through his holy prophets he promised of old
     that he would save us from our enemies,
     and from the hands of all who hate us.

He promised to show mercy to our ancestors
     and to remember his holy covenant.

This was the oath he swore to our father Abraham:
     to set us free from the hands of our enemies,
free to worship him without fear,
     holy and righteous in his sight
     all the days of our life.

You, my child, shall be called the prophet of the
>   Most High;
>> for you will go before the Lord to prepare
>>   his way,
> to give his people knowledge of salvation
>> by the forgiveness of their sins.

In the tender compassion of our God
>   the dawn from on high shall break upon us,
> to shine on those who dwell in darkness and the
>>   shadow of death,
>> and to guide our feet into the way of peace.

Glory to the Father, and to the Son,
>   and to the Holy Spirit:
> as it was in the beginning, is now,
>>   and will be for ever. Amen.

Antiphon   Receive the Holy Spirit.
When you forgive sins, they are
forgiven, alleluia!

Prayer

Holy Spirit of truth,
Sovereign Lord of the universe,
guide and guardian of your people,
present everywhere,
overflowing all that exists:
Come and dwell in us,

cleanse us from all sin,
pour out your blessings on us,
give us fresh life,
and in your gracious love
bring us to salvation.
—Amen.

Text: Byzantine Liturgy.

Blessing

May the blessing of almighty God,
the Father, + the Son and the Holy Spirit,
descend upon us and remain with us for ever.
—Amen.

*****

The Role of the Holy Spirit

The Holy Spirit came down upon the Apostles, in the shape of *tongues*, to signify that he came to make them fit preachers of his word; and to endow them with the gift of *tongues*, accompanied with heavenly wisdom and understanding of the mysteries of God and all gospel truths; to the end that they might be enabled to teach and publish, throughout the whole world, the faith and law of Christ. And these *tongues* were of *fire*, to signify how this divine Spirit sets those souls on fire, in which he abides; enflaming them with divine love, consuming the dross of their earthly affections; putting them in a continual motion of earnest desires and endeavors, to go forward from virtue to virtue, as fire is always in motion; and carrying the upwards towards the God of gods in his heavenly Son; as the flame is always ascending upwards towards its element. O blessed fire, when shall I partake of your sacred flames? O come and take possession of my heart; consume all these bonds that tie it to the earth; and carry it up with you towards the heavenly furnace from whence you come. Sweet Jesus you said (Luke 12:49): "I am come to cast fire on the earth; and what will I but that it be kindled?" O cast this fire into my soul, that it may be kindled there!

Text: Bishop Richard Challoner (1691-1781) vicar apostolic of London (1741-1781), *Meditations for Ever Day in the Year* (London, 1767), vol. I, p. 311.

*****

Evening Prayer

O God, + come to my assistance.
—O Lord, make haste to help me.

Hymn

O Holy Spirit, by whose breath
life rises vibrant out of death:
come to create, renew, inspire;
come, kindle in our hearts your fire.

You are the seeker's sure resource,
of burning love the living source,
protector in the midst of strife,
the giver and the Lord of life.

In you God's energy is shown,
to us your varied gifts made known.
Teach us to speak, teach us to hear;
yours is the tongue and yours the ear.

Flood our dull senses with your light;
in mutual love our hearts unite.
Your power the whole creation fills;
confirm our weak, uncertain wills.

From inner strife grant us release;
turn nations to the ways of peace.
To fuller life your people bring
that as one body we may sing:

Praise to the Father, Christ his Word,
and to the Spirit, God the Lord;
to them all honor, glory be
both now and for eternity.
Amen.

Text: *Veni, Creator Spiritus*, attributed to Rabanus Maurus (776-865), trans.
John Webster Grant.

Psalm 121   The Spirit Our Protector

Antiphon   Wind and tongues of fire *
                fell on Mary and the apostles.

I look to the mountains;
where will my help come from?
My help will come from the Lord,
who made heaven and earth.

He will not let you fall;
your protector is always awake.
The protector of Israel never dozes or sleeps.
The Lord will guard you;
he is by your side to protect you.
The sun will not hurt you during the day,
nor the moon during the night.

The Lord will protect you from all danger;
he will keep you safe.
He will protect you as you come and go,
now and forever.

Antiphon   Wind and tongues of fire
                fell on Mary and the apostles.

Psalm Prayer

> God our Father,
> let the Spirit you sent on your Church
> to begin the teaching of the gospel
> continue to work in the world
> through the hearts of all who believe.
> We make our prayer through Christ our Lord.
> —Amen.

Reading

"The Spirit of wisdom and understanding, the Spirit of counsel and strength, the Spirit of knowledge and the fear of God" (Isaiah 11:2) came down upon the Lord and the Lord in turn gave this Spirit to his Church, sending the Advocate from heaven into all the world into which, according to his words, the devil too had been cast down like lightning. If we are not to be scorched and made unfruitful, we need the dew of God. Since we have our accuser, we need an Advocate as well. And so the Lord in his pity for us, who had fallen into the hands of brigands, having himself bound up our wounds and left for our care two coins bearing the imperial image, entrusted us to the Holy Spirit. Now, through the Spirit, the image and inscription of the Father and the Son have been given to us, and it is our duty to use the coin committed to our charge and make it yield a rich profit for the Lord.

Text: St. Irenaeus of Lyons (d. 203), *Against Heresies* 3, 17.

Response

When the Spirit of truth comes,
—He will lead you into all truth.

Canticle of Mary   Luke 1:46-55

Antiphon   Come, Holy Spirit, * fill the hearts of
your faithful
and kindle in them the fire of your
love, alleluia!

My soul + proclaims the greatness of the Lord,
my spirit rejoices in God my Savior;
for he has looked with favor on his lowly servant.

From this day all generations will call me blessed:
the Almighty has done great things for me,
and holy is his Name.

He has mercy on those who fear him
in every generation.

He has shown the strength of his arm,
he has scattered the proud in their conceit.

He has cast down the mighty from their thrones,
and has lifted up the lowly.

He has filled the hungry with good things,
and the rich he has sent away empty.

He has come to the help of his servant Israel
for he has remembered his promise of mercy,
the promise he made to our ancestors,
to Abraham and his children for ever.

Glory to the Father, and to the Son,
and to the Holy Spirit:
as it was in the beginning, is now,
and will be for ever. Amen.

Antiphon   Come, Holy Spirit, fill the hearts of
your faithful and kindle in them the
fire of your love, alleluia!

Litany to the Holy Spirit

Lord and life-giving Spirit,
you brooded over the primeval waters.
—Come, fill our hearts.

You led your people out of slavery in Egypt
and into the freedom of the promised land.
—Come, fill our hearts.

You overshadowed Mary of Nazareth
and made her the Mother of God.
—Come, fill our hearts.

You anointed Jesus as Messiah
when he was baptized by John in the Jordan.
—Come, fill our hearts.

You raised Jesus out of death
and proclaimed him Son of God in all his power.
—Come, fill our hearts.

You appeared on Pentecost in tongues of flame
and endowed your Church with charismatic gifts.
—Come, fill our hearts.

You send us out to testify to the Good News
about Jesus Christ.
—Come, fill our hearts.

Prayer

God of fire and light,
on the first Pentecost,
you formed the hearts
of those who believed in you
by the indwelling of the Holy Spirit:
Under the inspiration of that same Spirit
give us a taste for what is right and true

and a continuing sense
of his joy-bringing presence and power;
through Christ Jesus our Lord.
—Amen.

Blessing

May the grace of our Lord Jesus Christ
+ and the love of God,
and the fellowship of the Holy Spirit
be with us all for ever.
—Amen.

Tuesday—All Saints

Morning Prayer

O Lord, + open my lips.
—And my mouth will proclaim your praise.
How wonderful is God in all his saints.
—Come let us adore the Holy One.

Hymn

Lord God, we give you thanks for all your saints,
who sought the trackless footprints of your feet,
who took into their own a hand unseen
and heard a voice whose silence was complete.

In every word and deed they spoke of Christ,
and in their life gave glory to his name:
their love was unconsumed, a burning bush
of which the Holy Spirit was the flame.

Blest Trinity, may yours be endless praise
for all who lived so humbly in your sight:
your holy ones who walked dark ways in faith
now share the joy of your unfailing light. Amen.

Text: *The Stanbrook Abbey Hymnal*, rev. ed., © 1974 Stanbrook Abbey
Music, Worcester, U.K.

Psalm 24a   The Saints in the Presence of God

Antiphon   Happy are the pure in heart; *
            they will see God.

The world and all that is in it belong to the Lord;
the earth and all who live on it are his.
He built it on the deep waters beneath the earth
and laid its foundations in the ocean depths.

Who has the right to go up the Lord's hill?
Who may enter his holy Temple?
Those who are pure in act and in thought,
who do not worship idols
or make false promises.

The Lord will bless them and save them;
God will declare them innocent.
Such are the people who come to God,
who come into the presence of the God of Jacob.

Antiphon   Happy are the pure in heart;
            they will see God.

Psalm Prayer

God of all holiness,
you are glorified in the assembly of the saints
and in crowning their merits
you are but crowning your own gifts.
Surrounded by such a crowd of witnesses,
help us run our appointed race
and with them receive a never-fading garland of glory,
through Jesus Christ our Lord.
—Amen.

Reading   Micah 6:8

The Lord has told us what is good. What he requires
of us is this: to do what is just, to show constant love, and
to live in humble fellowship with our God.

Response

The righteous shall praise your name, O Lord.
—The upright shall walk in your presence.

Canticle of Zachary   Luke 1:68-79

Antiphon   The just will shine like the sun *
in the kingdom of their Father.

Blessed be + the Lord, the God of Israel;
    he has come to his people and set them free.
He has raised up for us a mighty Savior,
    born of the house of his servant David.

Through his holy prophets he promised of old
    that he would save us from our enemies,
    and from the hands of all who hate us.

He promised to show mercy to our ancestors
    and to remember his holy covenant.

This was the oath he swore to our father Abraham:
    to set us free from the hands of our enemies,
free to worship him without fear,
    holy and righteous in his sight
    all the days of our life.

You, my child, shall be called the prophet of
    the Most High;
    for you will go before the Lord to prepare his way,
to give his people knowledge of salvation
    by the forgiveness of their sins.

In the tender compassion of our God
    the dawn from on high shall break upon us,
to shine on those who dwell in darkness and the
    shadow of death,
    and to guide our feet into the way of peace.

Glory to the Father, and to the Son,
  and to the Holy Spirit:
as it was in the beginning, is now,
  and will be for ever. Amen.

Antiphon   The just will shine like the sun
            in the kingdom of their Father.

Prayer

Almighty and ever-living God,
you kindled the flame of love
in the hearts of your saints.
Give us the same power of faith and love
that, as we rejoice in their triumphs,
we may profit by their example and their prayers.
We ask this through Christ our Lord.
—Amen.

Blessing

May Christ, the King of glory,
+ grant us his peace.
—Amen.

*****

The Heavenly Liturgy

In the earthly liturgy, by way of foretaste, we share in that heavenly liturgy which is celebrated in the holy city of Jerusalem toward which we journey as pilgrims, and in which Christ is sitting at the right hand of God, a minister of the sanctuary and of the true tabernacle; we sing a hymn to the Lord's glory with all the warriors of the heavenly army; venerating the memory of the saints, we hope for some part and fellowship with them; we eagerly await the Savior, our Lord Jesus Christ, until he, our life, shall appear and we too will appear with him in glory.

Text: Constitution of the Sacred Liturgy, 8, trans. Walter M. Abbott, S.J. *The Documents of Vatican II* (The America Press, 1966), pp. 141-142

The Example of the Saints

In order to build up our faith, to confirm our hearts, and to enlighten our awareness in faith, let us prudently look to those great lights of the Church, the men and women of great spiritual knowledge, wisdom, and proven holiness, and to their teaching and writings, their works and martyrdoms. Let us say to ourselves against the movements of our own temptations: Are you really better than they are, holier, wiser, sharper, than those who have taught the world what they have learned from the Lord? They preached it magnificently. They handed it down to us in rich descriptions. They have confirmed it by their lives and miracles and have made it holy by their deaths and martyrdoms.

Text: William of St. Thierry, *The Way to Divine Union*, ed. M. Basil Pennington, O.C.S.O. (Hyde Park, NY: New City Press), p. 117.

*****

Evening Prayer
O God, + come to my assistance.
—O Lord, make haste to help me.

Hymn
O white-robed King of glory,
you come to seek your own;
with angel hosts around you,
you claim your altar throne.
A hundred-thousand welcomes
we give you, God most high;
with loving hearts we greet you,
high King of earth and sky.

You come yourself to bring us
the hope of Paradise;
you come to lead us homeward
to joy beyond the skies.

You come in hidden glory
who yet will come again
in majesty and splendor
to be our great Amen.

O King of kings, in wonder
we wait for that blest morn,
new springtime of creation,
when all shall be reborn.
Then by your Word almighty
the promised heaven and earth
in glory and in gladness
at last shall come to birth.

Text: James Quinn, S.J., *Praise for All Seasons*, (Kingston, NY: Selah Publishing, 1994), p. 93.

Psalm 145   One Universal Act of Praise

Antiphon   Worship the Lord * in the
beauty of holiness.

I will proclaim your greatness, my God and king;
I will thank you forever and ever.
Every day I will thank you;
I will praise you forever and ever.
The Lord is great and is to be highly praised;
his greatness is beyond understanding.

What you have done will be praised
from one generation to the next;
they will proclaim your mighty acts.
They will speak of your glory and majesty,
and I will meditate on your wonderful deeds.
People will speak of your mighty deeds,
and I will proclaim your greatness.

They will tell about all your goodness
and sing about your kindness.
The Lord is loving and merciful,
slow to become angry and full of constant love.
He is good to everyone
and has compassion on all he made.

All your creatures, Lord, will praise you,
and all your people will give you thanks.
They will speak of the glory of your royal power
and tell of your might,
so that everyone will know your mighty deeds
and the glorious majesty of your kingdom.
Your rule is eternal,
and you are king forever.

Antiphon   Worship the Lord in the beauty
of holiness.

Psalm Prayer

Heavenly Father,
as we rejoice with the holy men and women
of every age and race,
may we receive from you
the fullness of forgiveness
we have always desired.
Please grant this through Christ our Lord.
—Amen.

Reading   Revelation 7:9-10, 12

I looked and there was an enormous crowd—no one could count all the people! They were from every race, tribe, nation, and language, and they stood in front of the throne and of the Lamb, dressed in white robes and holding palm branches in their hands. They called out in a loud voice: "Salvation comes from our God, who sits on the throne and from the Lamb. . . . Amen! Praise, glory, wisdom, thanksgiving, honor, power, and might belong to our God forever and ever! Amen!"

Response

Let God's people rejoice in their triumph,
—And sing joyfully at their feasts.

Canticle of Mary   Luke 1:46-55

Antiphon   The whole company of heaven *
              proclaims your glory, O Blessed
              Trinity, one God!

My soul + proclaims the greatness of the Lord,
my spirit rejoices in God my Savior
for he has looked with favor on his lowly servant.

From this day all generations will call me blessed:
the Almighty has done great things for me,
and holy is his Name.

He has mercy on those who fear him
in every generation.

He has shown the strength of his arm,
he has scattered the proud in their conceit.

He has cast down the mighty from their thrones,
and has lifted up the lowly.

He has filled the hungry with good things,
and the rich he has sent away empty.

He has come to the help of his servant Israel
for he has remembered his promise of mercy,
the promise he made to our ancestors,
to Abraham and his children for ever.

Glory to the Father, and to the Son,
    and to the Holy Spirit:
as it was in the beginning, is now,
    and will be for ever. Amen.

Antiphon   The whole company of heaven
                    proclaims your glory, O Blessed
                    Trinity, one God!

Litany (see the Byzantine Litany, pp. 310-313) or this prayer

Almighty and ever-living God,
by your grace
we live in communion with all your saints.
By their prayers
make us true disciples of your Son
during our earthly pilgrimage,
and in our heavenly home
let us share their fullness of joy,
through Jesus Christ our Lord.
—Amen.

Blessing

May Jesus Christ, the Lord of all the saints,
+ bless us and keep us.
—Amen.

All Souls (An Alternative to All Saints)

Morning Prayer

O Lord, + open my lips.
—And my mouth will proclaim your praise.
Come, let us worship the Lord.
—All things live for him.

Hymn

O Lord, you died that all might live
And rise to see the perfect day.
The fullness of your mercy give
To these our friends for whom we pray.
O Lamb of God, Redeemer blest,
Grant them eternal light and rest.

Lord, bless our friends who died in you,
As you have given them release.
Enliven them since they were true,
And give them everlasting peace.
O Lamb of God, Redeemer blest,
Grant them eternal light and rest.

In your green, pleasant pastures feed
The Sheep that you have summoned hence;
And by the still, cool waters lead

Your flock in loving providence.
O Lamb of God, Redeemer blest,
Grant them eternal light and rest.

Text: Richard F. Littledale (1833-1890), alt.

Psalm 27a   Confidence in God's Unfailing Help

Antiphon   O God, my Savior, * hear me when I
call to you.

The Lord is my light and my salvation;
I will fear no one.
The Lord protects me from all danger;
I will never be afraid.

When evil people attack me
and try to kill me,
they stumble and fall.
Even if a whole army surrounds me,
I will not be afraid;
even if enemies attack me,
I will still trust in God.

I have asked the Lord for one thing;
one thing only do I want:
to live in the Lord's house all my life,

to marvel there at his goodness,
and to ask for his guidance.

In times of trouble he will shelter me;
he will keep me safe in his Temple
and make me secure on a high rock.
So I will triumph over my enemies around me.
With shouts of joy I will offer sacrifices in
       his Temple;
I will sing, I will praise the Lord.

Give them eternal rest, O Lord,
and may your light shine on them forever.

Antiphon   O God, my Savior, hear me when I
                call to you.

Psalm Prayer
Father of Jesus, our risen Lord,
be our light and our salvation,
keep us safe in your Temple
and enable us to praise you,
now and for ever.
—Amen.

Reading   Wisdom 1:13–16
God did not invent death, and when living creatures die, it gives him no pleasure. He created everything so

that it might continue to exist, and everything he created
is wholesome and good. There is no deadly poison in
them. No, death does not rule this world, for God's justice
does not die. Ungodly people have brought death on
themselves by the things they have said and done. They
yearn for death as if it were a lover. They have gone into
partnership with death, and it is just what they deserve.

Response

Holy is God, holy and strong,
—Holy and living for ever.

Canticle of Zachary Luke 1:68-79 (see p. 148)

Antiphon   I am the resurrection and the life. *
Those who believe in me will live,
even though they die;
and those who live and believe in me
will never die!
Alleluia!

Prayer

O God, our Creator and Redeemer,
by your power Christ conquered death
and returned to you in glory.
May all your people who have gone before us in faith
share his victory and enjoy the vision of your
glory for ever.

We make our prayer through Jesus our Lord.
—Amen.
For additional prayers see p. 143

Blessing

May the souls of the faithful departed
through the mercy of God + rest in peace.
—Amen.

*****

Christ the Conqueror of Death

Let no one fear death, for the Savior's death
        has set us free.
He who was held prisoner by death has annihilated it.
By descending into death he has taken death captive.
He angered it when death tasted of his flesh.
The Prophet Isaiah saw this and cried out:
"Death was angered when it encountered you
    in the nether regions."
Death was angered, for it was defeated.
Death was angered, for it was mocked.
Death was angered, for it was abolished.
Death was angered, for it was overthrown.
Death was angered, for it was bound in chains.

O Death, where is your sating?
O Grave, were is your victory?
Christ is risen and you are overthrown.
Christ is risen and the devils have fallen.
Christ is risen and the angels rejoice.
Christ is risen and life is set free.
Christ is risen and not one dead person
    remains in the grave.
For Christ, now raised from the dead,
    has become the first-fruits
    of those who have fallen asleep in death,
    and to him be glory and honor,
    now and always and for ever and ever.
        Amen.

Text: St. John Chrysostom (ca. 347-407), *Homily for the Vigil of Easter*.

*****

Evening Prayer

O God, + come to my assistance.
—O Lord, make haste to help me.

Hymn

All you who seek a comfort sure
In sadness and distress,
Whatever sorrow burdens you,

Whatever griefs oppress:
When Jesus gave himself for us
And died upon the tree,
His heart was pierced for love of us;
He died to set us free.

Now hear him as he speaks to us
Those words for ever blest:
"All you who labor come to me,
And I will give you rest."
O heart adored by saints on high,
And hope of sinners here,
We place our ev'ry trust in you
And lift to you our prayer.

Text: *Quicumque certum quaertis*, Latin, eighteenth century, trans. Edward Caswall (1814-1878), alt.

Psalm 130   A Plea for Mercy and Forgiveness

Antiphon   Trust in the Lord * because his love
              is constant.

From the depths of my despair
I call to you, Lord.
Hear my cry, O Lord;
listen to my call for help!

If your kept a record of our sins,
who could escape being condemned?
But you forgive us,
so that we should stand in awe of you.

I wait eagerly for the Lord's help,
and in his word I trust.
I wait for the Lord
more eagerly than sentries wait for the dawn—
than sentries wait for the dawn.

Israel, trust in the Lord,
because his love is constant
and he is always willing to save.
He will save his people Israel
from all their sins.

Grant them eternal rest, O Lord,
and may your light shine on them forever.

Antiphon   Trust in the Lord because his love
            is constant.

Psalm Prayer

God of love,
have mercy on our brothers and sisters who
        have died.

May their faith and hope in you
be rewarded by eternal life.
We ask this through Christ our Lord.
—Amen.

Reading   Revelation 14:13

I heard a voice from heaven saying, "Write this:
Happy are those who from now on die in the service of
the Lord!" "Yes, indeed!" answers the Spirit. "They will
enjoy rest from their hard work, because the results of
their service go with them."

Response

Heaven is our home
—As we eagerly await the coming of our Savior.

Canticle of Mary   Luke 1:46-55 (see p. 154)

Antiphon   I am the bread of life. * Anyone who
eats this bread will live for ever.

Litany for the Faithful Departed

By the precious blood shed
    when you were circumcised
and became a child of Israel.
—Grant them rest and peace.

By the precious blood that dropped to the ground
during your agony in the Garden of Gethsemane.
—Grant them rest and peace.

By the precious blood that flowed from your limbs
when you were scourged at the pillar.
—Grant them rest and peace.

By the precious blood that ran down your head and face
when you were cruelly crowned with thorns.
—Grant them rest and peace.

By the precious blood that spilled to the ground
as you walked to Golgotha.
—Grant them rest and peace.

By the precious blood that issued from
your hands and feet when you were nailed
        to the cross.
—Grant them rest and peace.

By the water and the precious blood that
        poured forth
from your heart pierced by a lance.
—Grant them rest and peace.

(spontaneous prayer)

Prayers

Father of all consolation,
source of forgiveness and salvation for all,
hear our prayer.
By the intercession of the Blessed Virgin Mary,
may our friends, relatives, and benefactors
who have gone from this world
come to share eternal happiness with all your saints.
Please grant this through Christ our Lord.
—Amen.

For One Person

Almighty God, our Father,
we firmly believe that your Son died and rose to life.
We pray for our brother (sister) *Name,*
who has died in Christ.
Raise him (her) at the last day
to share the glory of the risen Christ,
who lives and reigns with you and the Holy Spirit,
one God, for ever and ever.
—Amen.

For an Anniversary

God of mercy,
we keep this anniversary
of the death (burial) of *Name,* our sister (brother).
Give her (him) light, happiness and peace.

We ask this through Christ our Lord.
—Amen.

Blessing

May the souls of the faithful departed
through the mercy of God + rest in peace.
—Amen.

In the twilight of life, God will not judge us on our earthly possessions and human success, but rather on how much we have loved.

St. John of the Cross (1542-1591)

Wednesday—St. Joseph

Morning Prayer
O Lord, + open my lips.
—And my mouth will proclaim your praise.
Let us praise Christ the Lord,
—As we celebrate the memory of St. Joseph.

Hymn
By all your saints still striving,
For all your saints at rest,
Your holy name, O Jesus,
For evermore be blessed.
You rose our king victorious,
That they might wear the crown
And ever shine in splendor
Reflected from your throne.

All praise, O God, for Joseph,
The guardian of your Son,
Who saved him from King Herod,
When safety there was none.
He taught the trade of builder,
When they to Nazareth came,
And Joseph's love made "Father"
To be, for Christ, God's name.

Then let us praise the Father
And worship God the Son
And sing to God the Spirit,
Eternal Three in One,
Till all the ransomed number
Who stand before the throne,
Ascribe all power and glory
and praise to God alone.

Text: Horatio Bolton Nelson (1823-1913) alt. by Jerry D. Godwin (b. 1944), © New York: Church Pension Fund, 1982.

Psalm 92 God's Upright Servant

Antiphon Joseph was a man * who always did
what was right.

How good it is to give thanks to you, O Lord,
to sing in your honor, O Most High God,
to proclaim your constant love every morning
and your faithfulness every night,
with the music of stringed instruments
and with melody on the harp.
Your mighty deeds, O Lord, make me glad;
because of what you have done, I sing for joy.

How great are your actions, Lord!
How deep are your thoughts!
This is something a fool cannot know;

someone who is stupid cannot understand:
the wicked may grow like weeds,
those who do wrong may prosper;
yet they will be totally destroyed,
because you, Lord, are supreme forever.

The righteous will flourish like palm trees;
they will grow like the cedars of Lebanon.
They are like trees planted in the house of the Lord,
that flourish in the Temple of our God,
that still bear fruit in old age
and are always green and strong.
This shows that the Lord is just,
that there is no wrong in my protector.

Antiphon   Joseph was a man who always did
             what was right.

Psalm Prayer

Father,
you entrusted our Savior
to the care of St. Joseph.
By the help of his prayers
may your Church continue to serve its Lord,
Jesus Christ,
who lives with you and the Holy Spirit,
one God, for ever and ever.
—Amen.

Reading   Sirach 26:1-4

The husband of a good wife is a fortunate man; he will live twice as long because of her. A fine wife is a joy to her husband, and he can live out his years in peace. A good wife is among the precious blessings given to those who fear the Lord.

Response

Mary was engaged to a man called Joseph,
—a descendant of King David.

Canticle of Zachary   Luke 1:68-79

Antiphon   Joseph was a faithful and wise steward *
whom the Lord set over his family.

Blessed be + the Lord, the God of Israel;
he has come to his people and set them free.

He has raised up for us a mighty Savior,
born of the house of his servant David.

Through his holy prophets he promised of old
that he would save us from our enemies,
and from the hands of all who hate us.

He promised to show mercy to our ancestors
and to remember his holy covenant.

This was the oath he swore to our father Abraham:
to set us free from the hands of our enemies,
free to worship him without fear,
holy and righteous in his sight
all the days of our life.

You, my child, shall be called the prophet of
the Most High;
for you will go before the Lord to prepare his way,
to give his people knowledge of salvation
by the forgiveness of their sins.

In the tender compassion of our God
the dawn from on high shall break upon us,
to shine on those who dwell in darkness and the
shadow of death,
and to guide our feet into the way of peace.

Glory to the Father, and to the Son,
and to the Holy Spirit:
as it was in the beginning, is now,
and will be for ever. Amen.

Antiphon   Joseph was a faithful and wise steward
whom the Lord set over his family.

Prayer

God,
in your infinite wisdom and love
you chose Joseph to be the husband of Mary,
the mother of your Son.
May we who enjoy his protection of earth
have his prayers to help us in heaven.
We ask this through Christ our Lord.
—Amen.

Blessing

May the Word made flesh,
full of grace and truth,
+ bless us and keep us.
—Amen.

*****

Prayer to St. Joseph

Good St. Joseph,
ever-watchful guardian of the holy family,
protect the chosen people of Jesus Christ,
keep us free from the blight of error and corruption,
and be our ally in the conflict with the powers
of darkness.
As of old you rescued the child Jesus from the plots
of Herod,
so now defend the universal Church from all harm.

Keep us one and all under your continual protection,
so that by your help and example,
we may lead a holy life, die a godly death,
and attain to a happy eternity in heaven.
—Amen.

*****

Evening Prayer
O God, + come to my assistance.
—O Lord, make haste to help me.

Hymn
Joseph, we praise you, prince of God's
      own household,
Bearing the promise made of old to David,
Chosen to foster Christ, the Lord's anointed,
Son of the Father.

Strong in your silence, swift in your obedience,
Saving God's firstborn when you fled from Herod,
Cherish God's children as you cherished Jesus,
Safe in your keeping.

Saint of the workbench, skilled and
      trusted craftsman,
Cheerfully toiling side by side with Jesus,

Teach us to value lives of hidden splendor,
Lived in God's presence.

Husband of Mary, one in joy and sorrow,
Share with God's people love and peace and blessing;
May your example help our homes to mirror
Nazareth's glory.

Saint of the dying, when your work was ended
Jesus and Mary stood beside your deathbed;
So in life's evening may they stand beside you,
Calling us homeward.

Text: James Quinn, S.J., *Praise for All Seasons*, (Kington, NY: Selah
Publishing, 1994) p. 106.

Psalm 1   True Happiness

Antiphon   Happy are those who are humble; *
                 they will receive what God has promised.

Happy are those who reject the advice of evil people,
who do not follow the example of sinners
or join those who have no use for God.
Instead, they find joy in obeying the Law of the Lord,
and they study it day and night.
They are like trees that grow beside a stream,

that bear fruit at the right time,
and whose leaves do not dry up.
They succeed in everything they do.

But evil people are not like this at all;
they are like straw that the wind blows away.
Sinners will be condemned by God
and kept apart from God's own people.
The righteous are guided and protected by the Lord,
but the evil are on the way to their doom.

Antiphon   Happy are those who are humble;
             they will receive what God has promised.

Psalm Prayer

God our Father,
Creator and Ruler of the universe,
in every age you call us
to develop and use our gifts
for the good of others.
With St. Joseph as our example and guide,
help us to do the work you have asked
and come to the rewards you have promised.
Please grant this through Christ our Lord.
—Amen.

Reading   Colossians 3:23-24

Whatever you do, work at it with all your heart, as though you were working for the Lord and not for people. Remember that the Lord will give you as a reward what he has kept for his people. For Christ is the real Master you serve.

Response

Well done, good and faithful servant!
—Come and share my happiness.

Canticle of Mary   Luke 1:46-55

Antiphon   Joseph's name * will live through
all generations.

My soul + proclaims the greatness of the Lord,
my spirit rejoices in God my Savior;
for he has looked with favor on his lowly servant.

From this day all generations will call me blessed:
the Almighty has done great things for me,
and holy is his Name.

He has mercy on those who fear him
in every generation.

He has shown the strength of his arm,
he has scattered the proud in their conceit.

He has cast down the mighty from their thrones,
and has lifted up the lowly.

He has filled the hungry with good things,
and the rich he has sent away empty.

He has come to the help of his servant Israel
for he has remembered his promise of mercy,
the promise he made to our ancestors,
to Abraham and his children for ever.

Glory to the Father, and to the Son,
    and to the Holy Spirit:
as it was in the beginning, is now,
    and will be for ever. Amen.

Antiphon   Joseph's name will live through all
                generations.

Litany of St. Joseph (see p. 308-310)
or this prayer

Heavenly Father,
from the family of your servant David
you raised up Joseph to be the guardian
of your incarnate Son
and the spouse of his virgin mother.
Give us grace to imitate his uprightness of life
and his obedience to your commands,
through Jesus Christ our Lord.
—Amen.

Blessing

May Jesus, our incarnate God,
+ bless us and keep us.
—Amen.

Thursday—The Blessed Sacrament

Morning Prayer

O Lord, + open my lips.
—And my mouth will proclaim your praise.
Come, let us adore Christ the Lord, the bread of life.
—Come let us adore him.

Hymn

Hail our Savior's glorious body,
Which his Virgin Mother bore;
Hail the blood which, shed for sinners,
Did a broken world restore;
Hail the sacrament most holy,
Flesh and blood of Christ adore!

Come adore this wondrous presence;
Bow to Christ, the source of grace!
Here is kept the ancient promise
Of God's earthly dwelling-place!
Sight is blind before God's glory,
Faith alone may see his face!

Glory be to God the Father,
Praise to his coequal Son,
Adoration to the Spirit,

Bond of love, in Godhead one!
Blest be God by all creation
Joyously while ages run!
—Amen.

Text: *Pange, lingua, gloriosi cororis*, verses 1, 5-6, St. Thomas Aquinas, OP (1227-1274), trans. James Quinn, S.J., *Praise for All Seasons*, (Kingston, NY: Selah Publishing, 1994) p. 59.

Psalm 42   The Altar Is Our Home

Antiphon   I will go to your altar, O God; *
             you are the source of my happiness.

As a deer longs for a stream of cool water,
so I long for you, O God.
I thirst for you, the living God.
When can I go and worship in your presence?
Day and night I cry,
and tears are my only food;
all the time my enemies ask me,
"Where is your God?"

My heart breaks when I remember the past,
when I went with the crowds to the house of God
and led them as they walked along,
a happy crowd, singing and shouting praise to God.

Why am I so sad?
Why am I so troubled?
I will put my hope in God,
and once again I will praise him,
my Savior and my God.

May the Lord show his constant love during the day,
so that I may have a song at night,
a prayer to the God of my life.

Antiphon   I will go to your altar, O God;
              you are the source of my happiness.

Psalm Prayer
O God of presence and power,
in this life of exile
may the bread of life on our altars
relieve our sadness
and bring us rejoicing into your house,
singing and shouting your praises.
We ask this through Christ our Lord.
—Amen.

Reading   Malachi 1:11
From the rising of the sun to its setting my name is
great among the nations, and in every place incense is
offered to my name, and a pure offering; for my name is
great among the nations, says the Lord of hosts (NRSV).

159

Response

You gave them bread from heaven to be their food.
—And this bread contained all goodness.

Canticle of Zachary   Luke 1:68-79

Antiphon   I am the living bread * that came down
from heaven.
If you eat this bread, you will live forever.

Blessed be + the Lord, the God of Israel;
    he has come to his people and set them free.

He has raised up for us a mighty Savior,
    born of the house of his servant David.

Through his holy prophets he promised of old
    that he would save us from our enemies,
    and from the hands of all who hate us.

He promised to show mercy to our ancestors
    and to remember his holy covenant.

This was the oath he swore to our father Abraham:
    to set us free from the hands of our enemies,
free to worship him without fear,
    holy and righteous in his sight
    all the days of our life.

You, my child, shall be called the prophet of the
>   Most High;
>   for you will go before the Lord to prepare his way,
to give his people knowledge of salvation
>   by the forgiveness of their sins.

In the tender compassion of our God
>   the dawn from on high shall break upon us,
to shine on those who dwell in darkness and the
>   shadow of death,
>   and to guide our feet into the way of peace.

Glory to the Father, and to the Son,
>   and to the Holy Spirit:
as it was in the beginning, is now,
>   and will be for ever. Amen.

Antiphon   I am the living bread that came down
>   from heaven.
>   If you eat this bread, you will live forever.

Prayer

>   Lord Jesus Christ,
>   you gave us the Eucharist
>   as the memorial of your suffering and death.
>   May our worship of this sacrament
>   of your body and blood

help us to experience the salvation you won for us
and the peace of the kingdom,
where you live with the Father and the Holy Spirit,
one God, for ever and ever.
—Amen.

Blessing

May Christ, the bread of life,
+ be our strength and our stay.
—Amen.

*****

The Holy Eucharist

It was to impress the vastness of his love more firmly
on the hearts of the faithful that our Lord instituted this
sacrament at the Last Supper. As he was on the point of
leaving the world to go to the Father, after celebrating
the Passover with his disciples, he left it as a perpetual
memorial of his Passion. It was the fulfillment of the
ancient figures and the greatest of all his miracles, while
for those who were to experience the sorrow of his
departure, it was destined to be a unique and abiding
consolation.

Text: St. Thomas Aquinas, O.P. (1225-1274), *Opusculum* 57, 4.

*****

Evening Prayer

O God, + come to my assistance.
—O Lord, make haste to help me.

Hymn

The Word came into time and space,
yet never left his Father's side;
he came to do the work of grace
until, as night came down, he died.

His own disciple, faithless friend,
betrayed him, and the others fled;
but he had loved them to the end,
and feasted them on living bread.

And now, in these two outward signs
of bread and wine, these means of grace,
faith feeds on Christ himself and finds
enough for all the human race.

By being born, he shared our death,
to give us life that never dies;
reclaiming with his final breath
love's crowning glory as our prize.

Lord, through your sacrifice we thrive
as, flinging wide the gates of light,
you give us confidence to strive
against the warring hordes of night.

To you, with God in Trinity,
our everlasting praise is due;
so let us live eternally,
at home, triumphant Lord, with you.

Text: *Verbum supernum prodiens*, St. Thomas Aquinas, OP (1225-1274), trans.
Alan Gaunt, *The Hymn Texts of Alan Gaunt* (London: Stainer and Bell, 1991)
#87, pp. 113-114.

Psalm 111   The Memorial Meal

Antiphon   The Lord * never forgets his covenant.

With all my heart I will thank the Lord
in the assembly of his people.
How wonderful are the things the Lord does!

All who are delighted with them
want to understand them.
All he does is full of honor and majesty;
his righteousness is eternal.

The Lord does not let us forget his wonderful actions;
he is kind and merciful.
He provides food for those who honor him;
he never forgets his covenant.
He has shown his power to his people
by giving them the lands of foreigners.

In all he does he is faithful and just;
all his commands are dependable.
They last for all time;
they were given in truth and righteousness.
He set his people free
and made an eternal covenant with them.
Holy and mighty is he!

The way to become wise is to honor the Lord;
he gives sound judgment
to all who obey his commands.
He is to be praised forever.

Antiphon   The Lord never forgets his covenant.

Psalm Prayer
Kind and merciful Lord,
in the wonderful sacrament of the altar
you give us a living memorial of your dying
          and rising
and of the everlasting covenant established in
          your blood.
Keep us ever mindful of your wonderful actions
and faithful to your dependable commandments.
You live and reign for ever and ever.
—Amen.

Reading   1 Corinthians 10:16-17

The cup we use in the Lord's Supper and for which we give thanks to God: when we drink from it, we are sharing in the blood of Christ. And the bread we break: when we eat it, we are sharing in the body of Christ. Because there is the one loaf of bread, all of us, though many, are one body, for we all share the same loaf.

Response

The Lord gave them bread from heaven,
—Sending down manna for them to eat.

Canticle of Mary   Luke 1:46-55

Antiphon   How sacred is the feast *
in which Christ is our food,
the memorial of his passion
is celebrated anew,
our hearts are filled with grace,
and we are given a pledge
of the glory which is to come,
alleluia!

My soul + proclaims the greatness of the Lord,
my spirit rejoices in God my Savior;
for he has looked with favor on his lowly servant.

From this day all generations will call me blessed:
the Almighty has done great things for me,
and holy is his Name.

He has mercy on those who fear him
in every generation.

He has shown the strength of his arm,
he has scattered the proud in their conceit.

He has cast down the mighty from their thrones,
and has lifted up the lowly.

He has filled the hungry with good things,
and the rich he has sent away empty.

He has come to the help of his servant Israel
for he has remembered his promise of mercy,
the promise he made to our ancestors,
to Abraham and his children for ever.

Glory to the Father, and to the Son,
    and to the Holy Spirit:
as it was in the beginning, is now,
    and will be for ever. Amen.

The antiphon above is repeated.

Litany of the Blessed Sacrament
(see pp. 298-300)
or this prayer

Father,
for your glory and our salvation
you appointed Jesus Christ eternal high priest.
May the people he gained for you by his blood
come to share in the power of his cross
    and resurrection
by celebrating his memorial in the Eucharist,
for he lives and reigns with you and the Holy Spirit,
one God, for ever and ever.
—Amen.

Blessing

May Christ Jesus,
Son of God and Son of Mary,
+ bless us and keep us.
—Amen.

Friday—
The Sacred Heart of Jesus

Morning Prayer
O Lord, + open my lips.
—And my mouth will proclaim your praise.
Come, let us worship Jesus.
—Whose Heart was wounded for love of us.

Hymn
O sacred Heart, for all once broken,
Your precious blood for sinners shed,
Those words of love by you were spoken
That raised to life the living dead!

O Heart, your love for all outpouring
In pain upon the cross you bled;
Come now with life, our life restoring,
O Heart by which our hearts are fed!

Text: James Quinn, S.J., *Praise for All Seasons*, (Kingston, NY: Selah Publishing, 1994) p. 66.

Psalm 36b Jesus' Constant Goodness

Antiphon   How precious, * O Jesus, is your
constant love.

Lord, your constant love reaches the heavens;
your faithfulness extends to the skies.
Your righteousness is towering like the mountains;
your justice is like the depths of the sea.
People and animals are in your care.

How precious, O God, is your constant love!
We find protection under the shadow of your wings.
We feast on the abundant food your provide;
you let us drink from the river of your goodness.
You are the source of all life,
and because of your light we see the light.

Continue to love those who know you
and to do good to those who are righteous.
Do not let proud people attack me
or the wicked make me run away.

Antiphon   How precious, O Jesus, is your
constant love.

Psalm Prayer

Lord Jesus, living flame of love,
protect us under the wings of your cross
and be our constant source of light and life.
You live and reign for ever and ever.
—Amen.

Reading   Ephesians 2:4-8

God's mercy is so abundant, and his love for us so
great, that while we were spiritually dead in our disobe-
dience he brought us to life with Christ. It is by God's
grace that you have been saved. In our union with Christ
Jesus he raised us up with him to rule with him in the
heavenly world. He did this to demonstrate for all time
to come the extraordinary greatness of his grace in the
love he showed us in Christ Jesus. For it is by God's grace
that you have been saved through faith.

Response

Jesus is the Lamb of God
—who takes away the sins of the world.

Canticle of Zachary   Luke 1:68-79

Antiphon   In the tender compassion of our God *
we are saved by grace through faith.

Blessed be + the Lord, the God of Israel;
    he has come to his people and set them free.

He has raised up for us a mighty Savior,
    born of the house of his servant David.

Through his holy prophets he promised of old
    that he would save us from our enemies,
    and from the hands of all who hate us.

He promised to show mercy to our ancestors
    and to remember his holy covenant.

This was the oath he swore to our father Abraham:
    to set us free from the hands of our enemies,
free to worship him without fear,
    holy and righteous in his sight
    all the days of our life.

You, my child, shall be called the prophet of the
       Most High;
    for you will go before the Lord to prepare his way,
to give his people knowledge of salvation
    by the forgiveness of their sins.

In the tender compassion of our God
    the dawn from on high shall break upon us,

to shine on those who dwell in darkness and the
    shadow of death,
  and to guide our feet into the way of peace.

Glory to the Father, and to the Son,
  and to the Holy Spirit:
as it was in the beginning, is now,
  and will be for ever. Amen.

Antiphon   In the tender compassion of our God
             we are saved by grace through faith.

Prayer

Father, we rejoice in the gifts of love
we have received from the heart of Jesus your Son.
Open our hearts to share his life
and continue to bless us with his love.
We ask this through Christ our Lord.
—Amen.

Blessing

May the Heart of Jesus
+ be our light and our salvation.
—Amen.

*****

The opening in the side of Christ
reveals the riches of his love,
the love of his heart for us.

Text: St. Anselm of Canterbury (1033-1109)

Very merrily and gladly our Lord looked into his
side, and he gazed and said this: My child, if you cannot
look on my divinity, see here how I suffered my side to
be opened and my heart to be split in two and to send out
blood and water, all that was in it; and this is a delight to
me, and I wish it to be so for you. Our Lord showed this
to me to make us glad and merry.

Text: Julian of Norwich (1342-1416), *Showings,* 13, trans. Edmund
Colledge, OSA and James Walsh, SJ (New York: Paulist Press, 1978),
p. 146.

Your Savior comes not with gaudy show,
nor was his kingdom of the world below;
the crown he wore was of the pointed thorn,
in purple he was crucified not born.

Text: John Dryden (1631-1700).

*****

Evening Prayer
O God, + come to my assistance.
—O Lord, make haste to help me.

Hymn
Where true love is dwelling, God is dwelling there;
Love's own loving Presence love does ever share.

Love of Christ has made us out of many one;
In our midst is dwelling God's eternal Son.

Give him joyful welcome, love him and revere;
Cherish one another with a love sincere.

As in Christ we gather, discord has no part;
Ours is but one spirit, but one mind and heart.

Bitterness now ended, let there be accord;
Always with us dwelling be our God and Lord.

May we share the vision with the saints on high
Of Christ's matchless glory when we come to die.

Joy of all the blessed, be our heavenly prize;
Dwell with us for ever, Lord of Paradise!

Where true love is dwelling, God is dwelling there;
Love's own loving Presence love does ever share.

Text: *Ubi caritas,* trans. James Quinn, S.J., *Praise for All Seasons,* p. 62.

Psalm 103   God's Love in Jesus

Antiphon   His goodness * endures for
all generations.

Praise the Lord, my soul!
All my being praise his holy name!

Praise the Lord, my soul,
and do not forget how kind he is.
He forgives all my sins
and heals all my diseases.

He keeps me from the grave
and blesses me with love and mercy.
He fills my life with good things,
so that I stay young and strong like an eagle.

The Lord judges in favor of the oppressed
and gives them their rights.
The Lord is merciful and loving.
slow to become angry and full of constant love.
He does not keep on rebuking;
he is not angry for ever.
He does not punish us as we deserve
or repay us according to our sins and wrongs.

As high as the sky is above the earth,
so great is his love for those who honor him.
As far as the east is from the west,

so far does he remove our sins from us.
As a father is kind to his children,
so the Lord is kind to those who honor him.
He knows what we are made of;
he remembers that we are dust.

Praise the Lord, you strong and mighty angels,
who obey his commands,
who listen to what he says.
Praise the Lord, all you heavenly powers,
you servants of his, who do his will!
Praise the Lord, all his creatures
in all the places he rules.
Praise the Lord, my soul!

Antiphon   His goodness endures for
all generations.

Psalm Prayer

Lord our God,
open our hearts to the gentle rule of your Son,
our eternal priest and universal king.
May his kingdom of justice, peace, and love
establish its dominion everywhere.
We ask this through Jesus the Lord.
—Amen.

Reading   Romans 8:35, 37-39

Who can separate us from the love of Christ? Can trouble do it, or hardship or persecution or hunger or poverty or danger or death? No, in all these things we have complete victory through him who loved us! For I am certain that nothing can separate us from his love: neither death nor life, neither angels nor other heavenly rulers or powers, neither the present nor the future, neither the world above nor the world below—there is nothing in all creation that will ever be able to separate us from the love of God which is ours through Christ Jesus our Lord.

Response

My yoke is easy, says the Lord,
—my burden is light.

Canticle of Mary   Luke 1:46-55

Antiphon   One of the soldiers * plunged his spear
into Jesus' side,
         and at once blood and water poured out.

My soul + proclaims the greatness of the Lord,
my spirit rejoices in God my Savior
for he has looked with favor on his lowly servant.

From this day all generations will call me blessed:
the Almighty has done great things for me,
and holy is his name.

He has mercy on those who fear him
in every generation.

He has shown the strength of his arm,
he has scattered the proud in their conceit.

He has cast down the mighty from their thrones,
and has lifted up the lowly.

He has filled the hungry with good things,
and the rich he has sent away empty.

He has come to the help of his servant Israel
for he has remembered his promise of mercy,
the promise he made to our ancestors,
to Abraham and his children for ever.

Glory to the Father, and to the Son,
    and to the Holy Spirit:
as it was in the beginning, is now,
    and will be for ever. Amen.

Antiphon   One of the soldiers plunged his spear
               into Jesus' side,
                 and at once blood and water poured out.

Litany of the Sacred Heart of Jesus
(see pp. 295-297)
or this prayer
Father,
we honor the heart of your Son
broken by our cruelty,
yet symbol of love's triumph,
pledge of all that we are called to be.
Teach us to see Christ in the lives we touch,
to offer him living worship
by love-filled service to our brothers and sisters.
We ask this through Christ our Lord.
—Amen.

Text: Alternative opening Prayer, Feast of the Sacred Heart, *The Sacramentary*

Blessing
May the Heart of Jesus
+ be our life and our salvation.
—Amen.

Saturday—
The Blessed Virgin Mary

Morning Prayer
O Lord, + open my lips.
—And my mouth will proclaim your praise.
Come, let us adore Christ, the Son of Mary.
—Come, let us adore the Word made flesh.

Hymn   Maria Aurora
Mary the dawn, Christ the perfect Day.
Mary the gate, Christ the heavenly Way.

Mary the root, Christ the mystic Vine.
Mary the grape, Christ the sacred Wine.

Mary the wheat, Christ the living bread.
Mary the rose-bush, Christ the Rose blood-red.

Mary the font, Christ the cleansing Flood.
Mary the chalice, Christ the saving Blood.

Mary the temple, Christ the temple's Lord.
Mary the shrine, Christ the God adored.

Mary the beacon, Christ the haven's Rest.
Mary the mirror, Christ the Vision blest.

Mary the mother, Christ the mother's Son,
By all things blest while endless ages run. Amen.

Text: *Maria Aurora*, Paul Cross, 1949, sl. alt.

Canticle of Judith   13:18-20; 15:9; NRSV

Antiphon   Hail, Mary, * full of grace, the Lord is
with you.

O daughter, you are blessed by the Most High God
above all other women on earth.
And blessed be the Lord God,
who created the heavens and the earth,
who has guided you to cut off the head
of the leader of our enemies.

—Hail, Mary, full of grace, the Lord is with you.

Your praise will never depart from the hearts
of those who remember the power of God.
Blessed are you in every tent in Judah.

—Hail, Mary, full of grace, the Lord is with you.

May God grant this to be a perpetual honor to you,
and may he reward you with blessings,

because you risked your own life
when our nation was brought low,
and you averted our ruin,
walking in the straight path before our God.

—Hail, Mary, full of grace, the Lord is with you.

You are the glory of Jerusalem,
you are the great boast of Israel,
you are the great pride of our nation!

—Hail, Mary, full of grace, the Lord is with you.

Prayer

Most High God,
you have blessed a new heroine of Israel
above all other women on earth.
Mary risked her reputation and her life
by accepting your invitation
to be the Virgin-Mother of your only Son.
By her loving intercession
make us loyal and true to the gospel
of that same Son our Savior,
who lives and reigns with you and the Holy Spirit
one God, forever and ever.
—Amen.

Reading   Galatians 4:4-7

When the right time finally came, God sent his own Son. He came as the son of a human mother and lived under the Jewish Law, to redeem those who were under the Law, so that we might become God's children.

To show that you are his children, God sent the Spirit of his Son into our hearts, the Spirit who cries out, "Father, my Father." So then, you are no longer a slave but a child. And since you are his child, God will give you all that he has for his children.

Response

The Lord Almighty is determined
—to do all this.

Canticle of Zachary   Luke 1:68-79

Antiphon   Blessed are you among women, *
                O great Mother of God,
                Mary most holy!

Blessed be + the Lord, the God of Israel;
        he has come to his people and set them free.

He has raised up for us a mighty Savior,
        born of the house of his servant David.

Through his holy prophets he promised of old
    that he would save us from our enemies,
    and from the hands of all who hate us.

He promised to show mercy to our ancestors
    and to remember his holy covenant.

This was the oath he swore to our father Abraham:
    to set us free from the hands of our enemies,
free to worship him without fear,
    holy and righteous in his sight
    all the days of our life.

You, my child, shall be called the prophet of the
        Most High;
    for you will go before the Lord to prepare his way,
to give his people knowledge of salvation
    by the forgiveness of their sins.

In the tender compassion of our God
    the dawn from on high shall break upon us,
to shine on those who dwell in darkness and the
        shadow of death,
    and to guide our feet into the way of peace.

Glory to the Father, and to the Son,
and to the Holy Spirit:
as it was in the beginning, is now,
and will be for ever. Amen.

Antiphon   Blessed are you among women,
            O great Mother of God,
            Mary most holy!

Prayer

God our Father,
may we always have the prayers
of the Virgin Mother Mary,
for through Jesus Christ her Son
you bring us light and salvation;
he lives and reigns with you and the Holy Spirit,
one God, for ever and ever.
—Amen.

Blessing

May the Word made flesh,
full of grace and truth,
+ bless us and keep us.
—Amen.

*One difference between Christ and others is this:
they did not choose when to be born,
but he, the Lord and Maker of history, chose his time,
his birthplace, and his Mother.*

—St. Thomas Aquinas (1225-1274)

*****

Salutation to the Blessed Virgin Mary

Hail, O Lady,
holy Queen,
Mary, holy Mother of God:
you are the virgin made church
and the one
chosen by the most holy Father in heaven,
whom he consecrated
with his most holy beloved Son
and with the Holy Spirit the Paraclete,
in whom there was and is
all the fullness of grace and every good.
Hail, his Palace!
Hail, his Tabernacle!
Hail, his Home!
Hail, his Robe!
Hail, his Servant!
Hail, his Mother!
And hail, all you holy virtues,
which through the grace and light of the Holy Spirit
are poured into the hearts of the faithful
so that from their faithless state
you may make them faithful to God.

Text: St. Francis of Assisi (1181-1226), trans. Regis Armstrong, O.F.M. Cap. and Ignatius C. Brady, O.F.M., *Francis and Clare The Complete Works* (New York: Paulist Press, 1982), pp. 149-150.

*****

Evening Prayer

O God, + come to my assistance.
—O Lord, make haste to help me.

Hymn

Praise to Mary, heaven's gate,
Guiding star of Christians' way,
Mother of our Lord and King,
Light and hope to souls astray.

When you heard the call of God
Choosing to fulfill his plan,
By your perfect act of love
Hope was born in Adam's clan.

Help us to amend our ways,
Halt the devil's strong attack,
Walk with us the narrow path,
Beg for us the grace we lack.

Virgin chosen, singly blest,
Ever faithful to God's call,
Guide us in this earthly life,
Guard us lest, deceived, we fall.

Mary, help us live our faith
So that we may see your Son;

Join our humble prayers to yours,
Till life's ceaseless war is won.

Praise the Father, praise the Son,
Praise the Holy Paraclete;
Offer all through Mary's hands,
Let her make our prayers complete.
—Amen.

Text: *Ave maris stella*, Latin, ninth century, trans. Frank Quinn, O.P. et al.,
© World Library Publications.

Psalm 87   Mary, the Mother of All Nations

Antiphon   In Mary * is the source of all
            our blessings!

The Lord built his city on Zion, the sacred hill;
more than any other place in Israel
he loves the city of Jerusalem.
Listen, city of God,
to the wonderful things he says about you:

"I will include Egypt and Babylonia
when I list the nations that obey me;
the people of Philistia, Tyre, and Ethiopia
I will number among the inhabitants of Jerusalem."

Of Zion it will be said
that all nations belong there
and that the Almighty will make her strong.
The Lord will write a list of the peoples
and include them all as citizens of Jerusalem.
They dance and sing,
"In Zion is the source of all our blessings."

Antiphon   In Mary is the source of all
             our blessings!

Psalm Prayer
Lord God,
you made Mary your holy city,
the refuge of all who seek to obey you.
May we be numbered among her citizens
and dance and sing in her presence,
now and always and forever and ever.
—Amen.

Reading   Revelations 21:1-4
I, John, saw a new heaven and a new earth. The first
heaven and the first earth disappeared and the sea
vanished. And I saw the Holy City, the new Jerusalem,
coming down out of heaven from God, prepared and
ready, like a bride dressed to meet her husband. I heard
a loud voice speaking from the throne: "Now God's home
is with people! He will live with them, and they shall be

his people. God himself will be with them, and he will be their God. He will wipe away all tears from their eyes. There will be no more death, no more grief or crying or pain. The old things have disappeared."

Response

Blessed are you among women, O Virgin Mary,
—And blessed is the fruit of your womb, Jesus.

Canticle of Mary   Luke 1:46-55

Antiphon   We turn to you for protection,*
            holy Mother of God.
            Listen to our prayers
            and help us in our needs.
            Save us from every danger,
            glorious and blessed Virgin.

Tell out, + my soul, the greatness of the Lord;
Unnumbered blessings, give my spirit voice;
Tender to me the promise of his word;
In God my Savior shall my heart rejoice.

Tell out, my soul, the greatness of his name;
Make known his might, the deeds his arm has done;
His mercy sure, from age to age the same;
His holy name, the Lord, the Mighty One.

Tell out, my soul, the greatness of his might;
Powers and dominions lay their glory by,
Proud hearts and stubborn wills are put to flight,
The hungry fed, the humble lifted high.

Tell out, my soul, the glories of his word;
Firm is his promise, and his mercy sure,
Tell out, my soul, the greatness of the Lord
To children's children and for evermore.

Text: Timothy Dudley-Smith (1926-), copyright © in the USA The
Hope Publishing Company.

The antiphon above is repeated.

A Litany of the Blessed Virgin Mary
(see pp. 305-308)
or this prayer

Lord God,
give to your people the joy
of continual health in mind and body.
With the prayers of the Virgin Mary to help us
guide us through the sorrows of this life
to eternal happiness in the life to come.
Please grant this through Christ our Lord.
—Amen.

Blessing

May the Virgin Mary mild
+ bless us with her holy child.
—Amen.

To Jesus Through Mary

Our Lord looked down to his right, and brought to my mind where our Lady stood at the time of his Passion, and he said: Do you wish to see her? And I answered and said: Yes, good Lord, great thanks, if it be your will. Often times I had prayed for this, and I expected to see her bodily likeness; but I did not see her so. And Jesus, saying this, showed me a spiritual vision of her. Just as before I had seen her small and simple, now he showed her high and noble and glorious and more pleasing to him than all creatures. And so he wishes it to be known that all who take delight in him should take delight in her, and in the delight that he has in her and she in him. And when Jesus said: do you wish to see her? it seemed to me that I had the greatest delight that he could have given me, in this spiritual vision of her which he gave me. For our Lord showed me no particular person except our Lady, St. Mary, and he showed her to me on three occasions. The first was as she conceived, the second was as she had been in her sorrow under the cross, and the third as she is now, in delight, honor and joy.

And after this our Lord showed himself to me, and he appeared more glorified than I had ever seen him before, and in this I was taught that every contemplative soul to whom it is given to look and to seek Mary will pass on to God through contemplation.

Text: Julian of Norwich, *Showings* (Short text), trans. Edmund Colledge, O.S.A. and James Walsh, S.J. (New York: Paulist Press, 1978) pp. 147-148.

4. The Year of Our Lord

On the Lord's Day each week, we celebrate the Paschal Mystery in word and sacrament. It is "the original feast day, the foundation and kernel of the whole liturgical year" (Vatican II): The Lord's Supper on the Lord's Day for the Lord's People.

"The Week With Christ" celebrates seven key mysteries of Christ and his saints and may be used as the form of daily morning and evening prayer throughout the year.

In addition, by observing the special seasons of Advent/Christmas and Lent/Easter within the cycle of the Church's year, we let the whole mystery of Christ unfold before us: incarnation, birth, death, resurrection, ascension, pentecost, and parousia. Step by step we can meditate on and assimilate the inner meaning of the *one* mystery by reflecting on its many facets.

The cycle of the incarnation and the cycle of the passion, death, and resurrection are presented here in the poetry and prayer of the Catholic tradition. Like "The Week With Christ," each cycle has a form of Morning and Evening Prayer for the appropriate season.

Advent

Advent is a season of remembering and of longing. We remember the age-old prophecies of the coming Messiah, the angelic revelations to Mary and Joseph of Nazareth, the incarnation of the Word of God, and the role of John the Baptist in the initial preaching of the kingdom of God. In the light of what God has done in the Christmas mysteries, we long for their complete fulfillment in history and for the final coming of the Lord Jesus in glory to judge the living and the dead.

Advent begins with the Sunday on or nearest to the feast of St. Andrew, "the first-called," November 30, and lasts for nearly four weeks. It concludes on December 24, Christmas Eve.

See the Table of Movable Feasts, p. 411-412.

Morning Prayer

Blessed + is he who comes in the name of the Lord.
—Hosanna in the highest!

Hymn

Praise we the Lord this day,
This day so long foretold,
Whose promise shone with cheering ray
On waiting saints of old.

The prophet gave the sign
That those with faith might read;
A virgin, born of David's line
Shall bear the promised seed.

Blessed shall be her name
In all the Church on earth,
Through whom that wondrous mercy came,
The incarnate Savior's birth.

Jesus, the virgin's Son,
We praise you and adore,
Who are with God the Father one
And Spirit evermore. Amen.

Text: Anon., *Hymns for the Festivals and Saints' Days* (1846), alt.

Psalm 24:7-10   Christ Will Come Again in Glory

Antiphon   Who may enter * God's holy Temple?

Fling wide the gates,
open the ancient doors,
and the king of glory will come in!

Who is the great king?

He is the Lord Christ, strong and mighty,
the Lord Jesus, victorious in battle.

Fling wide the gates,
open the ancient doors,
and the great king of glory will come in!

Who is this great king?

He is our Lord Jesus Christ,
he is the Lord of Hosts,
he is the great king of glory!

Antiphon   Who may enter God's holy Temple?

Psalm Prayer

All-powerful God,
increase our strength of will for doing good
that Christ may find an eager welcome at his coming
and call us to his side in the kingdom of heaven,
where he lives and reigns with you
and the Holy Spirit,
one God, for ever and ever.
—Amen.

Reading   Isaiah 9:6-7

A child is born to us! A son is given to us! And he will be our ruler. He will be called, "Wonderful Counselor," "Mighty God," "Eternal Father," "Prince of Peace." His royal power will continue to grow; his kingdom will always be at peace.

Response

Let the clouds rain down the Just One,
—and the earth bring forth a Savior.

Canticle of Zephaniah   3:14-15, 17-18

Antiphon   The Lord * is in our midst.

Sing and shout for joy, people of Israel!
Rejoice with all your heart, Jerusalem!

The Lord has stopped your punishment;
he has removed all your enemies.
The Lord, the king of Israel, is with you;
there is no reason now to be afraid.

The Lord your God is with you;
his power gives you victory.
The Lord will take delight in you,
and in his love he will give you new life.
He will sing and be joyful over you,
as joyful as people at a festival.

Glory to the Father, and to the Son,
and to the Holy Spirit:
as it was in the beginning, is now,
and will be for ever. Amen.

Antiphon   The Lord is in our midst.

Prayer

Come, Lord Jesus,
do not delay.
Give new courage to your people
    who trust your love.
By your coming,
    raise us to the joy of your kingdom,
where you live and reign,

with the Father and the Holy Spirit,
one God, forever and ever.
—Amen.

Blessing

May our Savior,
coming on the clouds of heaven
with power and great glory,
+ bless us and keep us.
—Amen.

Evening Prayer

Our help + is in the name of the Lord,
—the maker of heaven and earth.

The Call

Come, my Way, my Truth, my Life:
Such a Way, as gives us breath:
Such a Truth, as ends all strife:
Such a Life, as killeth death.

Come, my Light, my Feast, my Strength:
Such a Light, as shows a feast:
Such a Feast, as mends in length:
Such a Strength, as makes his guest.

Come, my Joy, my Love, my Heart:
Such a Joy, as none can move:
Such a Love, as none can part
Such a Heart, as joys in Love.

Text: George Herbert (1593-1633)

Psalm 67   The Messianic Harvest

Antiphon   May all the peoples praise you, O God; *
may all the peoples praise you.

God be merciful to us and bless us;
look on us with kindness,
so that the whole world may know your will;
so that all nations may know your salvation.

May the peoples praise you, O God;
may all the peoples praise you!

May the nations be glad and sing for joy,
because you judge the peoples with justice
and guide every nation on earth.

May the peoples praise you, O God;
may all the peoples praise you!

The land has produced its harvest;
God, our God, has blessed us.
God has blessed us;
may all people everywhere honor him.

Antiphon   May all the peoples praise you, O God;
            may all the peoples praise you.

Psalm Prayer

As you came in our blessed Mother Mary
at the beginning of our salvation,
come now, Lord Jesus,
in our holy Mother, the Catholic Church,
and so prepare us for your final coming
at the end of time,
when you will reign in our hearts for ever.
—Amen.

Reading   Jeremiah 23:5-6

The Lord says, "The time is coming when I will choose as king a righteous descendant of David. That king will rule wisely and do what is right and just throughout the land. When he is king, the people of Judah will be safe, and the people of Israel will live in peace. He will be called 'The Lord Our Salvation.'"

Response

The Lord God will make him a king,
—as his ancestor David was.

Canticle of Mary Luke 1:46-55

Antiphon He will be called Emmanuel: *
God-is-with-us.

My soul + proclaims the greatness of the Lord,
my spirit rejoices in God my Savior;
for he has looked with favor on his lowly servant.

From this day all generations will call me blessed:
the Almighty has done great things for me,
and holy is his Name.

He has mercy on those who fear him
in every generation.

He has shown the strength of his arm,
he has scattered the proud in their conceit.

He has cast down the mighty from their thrones,
and has lifted up the lowly.

He has filled the hungry with good things,
and the rich he has sent away empty.

He has come to the help of his servant Israel
for he has remembered his promise of mercy,
the promise he made to our ancestors,
to Abraham and his children for ever.

Glory to the Father, and to the Son,
     and to the Holy Spirit:
as it was in the beginning, is now,
     and will be for ever. Amen.

Antiphon   He will be called Emmanuel:
             God-is-with-us.

Litany

Let us pray to the Lord who is coming to save us:
—Come and save us.
Lord Jesus, the Anointed of God,
—Come and save us.
You came forth from the Father into our world,
—Come and save us.
You were conceived by the power of the Spirit,
—Come and save us.
You took flesh in the womb of the Virgin Mary,
—Come and save us.
Savior of the living and the dead,
—Come and save us.

or Litany of the Holy Name of Jesus (pp. 292-295)

(spontaneous prayer)

Prayer

Heavenly Father,
you appointed your only-begotten Son
to be the Savior of the human race
and told his parents to call him Jesus.
May we who name him Savior now
come to see him face to face in heaven,
where he lives and reigns for ever and ever.
—Amen.

Blessing

May Christ Jesus, who is coming in glory
to judge the living and the dead,
+ bless us and keep us.
—Amen.

Marian Anthem for Advent

Mother of Christ, our hope, our patroness,
Star of the Sea, our beacon in distress,
Guide to the shores of everlasting day
God's holy people on their pilgrim way.

Virgin, in you God made his dwelling place;
Mother of all the living, full of grace,
Blessed are you: God's word you did believe,
"Yes" on your lips undid the "No" of Eve.

Daughter of God, who bore his holy One,
Dearest of all to Christ, your loving Son,
Show us his face, O Mother, as on earth,
Loving us all, you gave our Savior birth.

Text: *Alma Redemptoris Mater*, trans. James Quinn, S.J., *Praise for All Seasons* (Kingston, NY: Selah Pub., 1994), pp. 97.

Christmastide—December 25-February 2

The season of Christmas is a time of progressive revelations to the shepherds of Bethlehem, the Magi from the Orient, King Herod of Judea, John the Baptist and the first disciples, the wedding guests at Cana and, finally, to old Simeon and the prophetess Anna in the Temple. The mystery of Jesus' person and mission on earth gradually unfolds before the eyes of those who wish to see.

The feast of Christmas first appeared at Rome some years before 335. It was celebrated at the winter solstice, the ancient feast of the Undying Sun (*Sol Invictus*), the patronal feast of the Emperor Constantine before he and his family embraced Christianity. Little by little, it drew to itself the many other festivals that make up the Christmas season and celebrated them all in the greater light of the resurrection.

Morning Prayer

Blessed is he + who comes in the name of the Lord.
—Hosanna in the highest!

Hymn

To us a child of hope is born,
To us a son is given;
Him shall the tribes of earth obey,
Him all the hosts of heaven.

His name shall be the Prince of Peace,
For evermore adored,
The Wonderful, the Counselor,
The great and mighty Lord.

His power increasing still shall spread,
His reign no end shall know;
Justice shall guard his throne above
And peace abound below. Amen.

Text: Para. of Isaiah 9:2-8; from "The People that in Darkness Walked,"
John Morison (1750-1), *Scottish Translations and Paraphrases,* 1781, alt.

Psalm 2   God's Chosen Son, Our Messianic King

Antiphon   Today a Savior has been born to you, *
the Messiah and Lord.

Why do the nations plan rebellion?
Why do people make their useless plots?
Their kings revolt,
their rulers plot together against the Lord,
and against the king he chose.
"Let us free ourselves from their rule," they say;
"let us throw off their control."

From his throne in heaven the Lord laughs
and mocks their feeble plans.
Then he warns them in anger
and terrifies them with his fury.
"On Zion, my sacred hill," he says,
"I have installed my king."

"I will announce," says the king,
"what the Lord has declared.
He said to me: 'You are my son;
today I have become your father.
Ask, and I will give you all the nations;
the whole earth will be yours.
You will break them with an iron rod;
you will shatter them in pieces like a clay pot.'"

Now listen to this warning, you kings;
learn this lesson, you rulers of the world:
Serve the Lord with fear;
tremble and bow down to him;

or else his anger will be quickly aroused,
and you will suddenly die.
Happy are all who go to him for protection.

Antiphon   Today a Savior has been born to you,
            the Messiah and Lord.

Psalm Prayer

God of power and life,
glory of all who believe in you,
fill the world with your splendor
and show the nations the light of your truth.
We ask this through Christ our Lord.
—Amen.

Reading   Hebrews 1:1-3

In the past God spoke to our ancestors many times
and in many ways through the prophets, but in these last
days he has spoken to us through his Son. He is the one
through whom God created the universe, the one whom
God has chosen to possess all things at the end. He
reflects the brightness of God's glory and is the exact
likeness of God's own being, sustaining the universe with
his powerful word. After achieving forgiveness for the
sins of all human beings, he sat down in heaven at the
right side of God, the Supreme Power.

Response

The Lord has made known his salvation, alleluia!
—To all the ends of the earth, alleluia!

Canticle of the Word of God
John 1:1-5, 10-12, 14

Antiphon   Glory to God in the highest *
and peace to his people on
earth, alleluia!

In the beginning the Word already existed;
the Word was with God,
and the Word was God.
From the very beginning
the Word was with God.

Through him God made all things;
not one thing in all creation
was made without him.
The Word was the source of life,
and this life brought light to people.
The light shines in the darkness,
and the darkness has never put it out.

The Word was in the world,
and though God made the world through him,
yet the world did not recognize him.

He came to his own country,
but his own people did not receive him.
Some, however, did receive him
and believed in him;
so he gave them the right to become God's children.

The Word became a human being
and, full of grace and truth, lived among us.
We saw his glory,
the glory which he received as the Father's only Son.

Antiphon   Glory to God in the highest
            and peace to his people on
            earth, alleluia!

Prayer

Lord God,
we praise you for creating the human race
and still more for restoring it in Christ.
Your Son shared our weakness;
may we share his glory,
for he lives and reigns with you and the Holy Spirit,
one God, forever and ever.
—Amen.

Blessing

May the Word of God,
full of grace and truth,
+ bless us and keep us.
—Amen.

*****
Proclamation of the Nativity

Many ages after the creation of the world,
when God in the beginning made the heavens and
the earth,
long after the flood and the primeval covenant
with Noah,
more than two thousand years after the promises
made to our father Abraham and our mother Sarah,
fifteen centuries after Moses and Miriam
and the Exodus from Egypt,
one thousand years after David was anointed king
of Israel,
in the sixty-fifth week, according to the prophecy
of Daniel,
in the one hundred and ninety-fourth Olympiad,
in the year seven hundred and fifty-two
from the founding of the city of Rome,
in the forty-second year of the emperor
Augustus Caesar,
and in the sixth age of the world,
while the whole earth was at peace,
in order to consecrate the world by his coming,
JESUS CHRIST,
eternal God and Son of the eternal Father,
conceived in time by the power of the Holy Spirit,
nine months having elapsed since his conception,
was born of the Virgin Mary in Bethlehem of Judea,

GOD MADE MAN.
THIS THE BIRTHDAY ACCORDING TO THE FLESH
OF OUR LORD JESUS CHRIST.

Text: *The Roman Martyrology*, alt.

*****

Evening Prayer
Jesus Christ + is the true light
—That comes into the world and shines on all.

Poem   New Things and Old

The dark is shattered
With wild, new fear;
An ass's feet stumbling
Is the sound that I hear.

The night is brighter
Than day should be;
A strange star's splendor
Is the light that I see.

And above the terror
Of earth and sky
I can hear, if I listen,
A young Child's cry;

I can see if I look
Legions of wings,
And a woman who ponders
On all of these things.

Text: Sr. M. Madaleva, C.S.C. (1887-1964)

Psalm 110   Jesus: King, Priest, and Conqueror

Antiphon   I bring you good news of great joy: *
              A Savior is born for you today!

The Lord said to my lord,
"Sit here at my right side
until I put your enemies under your feet."

From Zion the Lord will extend your royal power.
"Rule over your enemies," he says.
On the day you fight your enemies,
your people will volunteer.
Like the dew of early morning
your young men will come to you on the sacred hills.

The Lord made a solemn promise
and will not take it back:
"You will be a priest for ever
in the priestly order of Melchizedek."

The Lord is at your right side;
when he becomes angry, he will defeat kings.
He will pass judgment on the nations
and fill the battlefield with corpses;
he will defeat kings all over the earth.
The king will drink from the stream by the road,
and strengthened, he will stand victorious.

Antiphon   I bring you good news of great joy:
              A Savior is born for you today!

Psalm Prayer

Lord Jesus Christ,
your birth is the joy of the whole world
as you come to do the will of him who sent you.
Be our high priest for ever,
protect the Church from its enemies
and quench our thirst for things eternal
with the fresh streams of your Spirit;
for yours is the kingdom, the power and the glory,
now and forever.
—Amen.

Reading   1 John 1:1-3

We write to you about the Word of life, which has existed from the very beginning. We have heard it, and we have seen it with our eyes; yes, we have seen it, and our hands have touched it. When this life became visible, we saw it; so we speak of it and tell you about the eternal life which was with the Father and was made known to us. What we have seen and heard we announce to you also, so that you will join with us in the fellowship that we have with the Father and with his Son Jesus Christ.

Response

The Word was made flesh, alleluia!
—And lived among us, alleluia!

Canticle of Mary   Luke 1:46-55

Antiphon   Today Christ is born, *
today the Savior has appeared,
today the angels are singing on earth,
the archangels are rejoicing,
today the saints exult and say:
Glory to God in the highest, alleluia!

My soul + proclaims the greatness of the Lord,
my spirit rejoices in God my Savior;
for he has looked with favor on his lowly servant.

From this day all generations will call me blessed:
the Almighty has done great things for me,
and holy is his Name.

He has mercy on those who fear him
in every generation.

He has shown the strength of his arm,
he has scattered the proud in their conceit.

He has cast down the mighty from their thrones,
and has lifted up the lowly.

He has filled the hungry with good things,
and the rich he has sent away empty.

He has come to the help of his servant Israel
for he has remembered his promise of mercy,
the promise he made to our ancestors,
to Abraham and his children for ever.

Glory to the Father, and to the Son,
    and to the Holy Spirit:
as it was in the beginning, is now,
    and will be for ever. Amen.

The above antiphon is repeated.

Te Deum Laudamus, part B

You, Christ are the king of glory,
—the eternal Son of the Father.
When you became man to set us free
—you did not spurn the Virgin's womb.
You overcame the sting of death,
—and opened the kingdom of heaven to
      all believers.
You are seated at God's right hand in glory.
—We believe that you will come, and be our judge.
Come, then, Lord, and help your people,
—bought with the price of your own blood.
And bring us with your saints
—to glory everlasting.

(spontaneous prayer)

Prayer

Christ our God,
fresh, new Adam of our springing hope!
Leaping down from the bosom of eternity,
issuing forth from the womb of new Eve,
     our Mother,
you are the light that cannot be extinguished.
O divine Word of God—
dressed in our very flesh and blood,
endued with our mortality,
you are the yoke-fellow of humanity,
the pilgrim, the stranger, the exile
in this death-dark vale of tears.
God-Man,
clasp us by the heart
and lead us at long last
to the home-haven of heaven,
where you live and reign, now and for ever.
—Amen.

Blessing

May Christ, the Son of God
and the Son of Mary,
+ bless us and keep us.
—Amen.

Marian Anthem for Christmastide

Mary of Bethlehem, crowned with heaven's glory,
Look on us, Mother, as we sing your praises;
Be with us always, joy of saints and angels,
Joy of creation.

Come to Christ's cave, all who serve Our Lady:
Sing to God's glory, young and old together,
Full hearts outpouring Mary's song of worship,
Thanking her Maker.

Sing to the Father, who exalts his handmaid;
Sing to God's wisdom, Son who chose his Mother;
Sing to their Spirit, Love that overshadowed
Mary, chaste Virgin.

Text: James Quinn, S.J., *Praise for All Seasons* (Kingston, NY: Selah Pub., 1994) p. 97, alt.

*****

A Christmas Devotion

1. Lord Jesus,
you proceeded from the heart
of the eternal Father
for our salvation
and were conceived
by the power of the Holy Spirit
in the womb of the Virgin Mother.

—Word made flesh, Emmanuel our God,
have mercy on us.

2. Lord Jesus,
by the visit of your Mother Mary
to her cousin Elizabeth,
John the Baptist, your herald and forerunner,
was filled with the Holy Spirit,
and danced for joy in his mother's womb.

—Word made flesh, Emmanuel our God,
have mercy on us.

3. Lord Jesus,
though by nature God,
you did not parade your equality with God
but became as a human being
and were enclosed for nine months
in Mary's womb.

—Word made flesh, Emmanuel our God,
have mercy on us.

4. Lord Jesus,
you were born in Bethlehem, the city of David,
you were wrapped in swaddling clothes
and laid in a manger;
you were heralded by angel choirs
and visited by wondering shepherds.

—Word made flesh, Emmanuel our God,
have mercy on us.

O Lord, the Virgin born to you
eternal praise and laud are due,
whom with the Father we adore
and Spirit blest for evermore.

Christ is now near to us, alleluia!
—Come let us adore him, alleluia!

5. Lord Jesus,
on the eighth day after your birth,
you were circumcised according to the Law
        of Moses,
and given the name Jesus,
the name revealed to Mary and Joseph
before your conception.

—Word made flesh, Emmanuel our God,
have mercy on us.

6. Lord Jesus,
by the leading of a star,
you were revealed to the Magi from the East
who adored you on Mary's lap
and honored you with mystical gifts:
gold, frankincense and myrrh.

—Word made flesh, Emmanuel our God,
have mercy on us.

7. Lord Jesus,
forty days after your birth,
your parents presented you in the Temple,
the aged Simeon received you into his arms
and Anna the prophetess revealed you to Israel.

—Word made flesh, Emmanuel our God,
have mercy on us.

8. Lord Jesus,
after the visit of the Magi,
an angel appeared to Joseph in a dream
and commanded him to escape into Egypt
with you and your Mother.

—Word made flesh, Emmanuel our God,
have mercy on us.

All glory, Jesus, be to you,
for evermore the Virgin's Son,
to Father and Paraclete
be praises while endless ages run!

Christ is born for us, alleluia!
—Come let us adore him, alleluia!

9. Lord Jesus,
your flight into Egypt snatched you from
        Herod's hands,
but a voice was heard in Ramah,
sobbing and lamenting,
Rachel weeping for her children,
because they were no more.

—Word made flesh, Emmanuel our God,
have mercy on us.

10. Lord Jesus,
after cruel Herod's death,
an angel again appeared to Joseph in a dream
and recalled you to the land of Israel,
where you made your home in Nazareth.

—Word made flesh, Emmanuel our God,
have mercy on us.

11. Lord Jesus,
in the humble home of Nazareth,
you lived in obedience to your parents,
were known as the carpenter's son
and grew in wisdom and in age
and in divine and human favor.

—Word made flesh, Emmanuel our God,
have mercy on us.

12. Lord Jesus,
when you were twelve years old,
at Passover you lingered in Jerusalem
and on the third day your parents found you in
        the Temple,
sitting among the teachers,
listening to them and asking them questions.

—Word made flesh, Emmanuel our God,
have mercy on us.

Mary, mother whom we bless,
full of grace and tenderness
defend me from the devil's power
and greet me in my dying hour.

—The Word was made flesh, alleluia!
And lived among us, alleluia!

Let us pray.
Almighty and everlasting God,
you reveal yourself to the little ones
and invite them into your Kingdom.
As we recall with devotion
the mysteries of your Son's childhood
and try to walk in his footsteps,
may we attain the Kingdom of heaven

he promised to those who receive it
as if they were little children.
We ask this through the same Christ our Lord.
— Amen.

Text: *Liber manualis minoritae*, ed. Donatus a Welle, O.F.M., Cap. (Rome: Desclée, 1931), pp. 98-101.

> *The thoughtfulness of Jesus and Mary and Joseph was so great that it made Nazareth the abode of God Most High. If we also have that kind of thoughtfulness for each other, our homes would really become the abode of God Most High.*

Text: Mother Teresa of Calcutta in Kathryn Spink (ed.), *Life in the Spirit* (San Francisco: Harper and Row Pub., 1983), p. 33.

Lent (40 Days)

Lent and Easter are one continuous season that celebrates in unique fashion the whole Paschal Mystery of Christ dying and rising in us. Lent prepares our catechumens for baptism/confirmation in the Easter Vigil and for their first Holy Communion on Easter morning. Lent also assists the already baptized to make a good annual confession of their sins in the sacrament of reconciliation so that they can renew their baptismal vows at Easter with faith and fervor.

Morning Prayer

O God, + come to my assistance.
—O Lord, make haste to help me.

Hymn

Eternal Lord of love, behold your Church
Walking once more the pilgrim way of Lent,
Led by your cloud by day, by night your fire,
Moved by your love and toward your presence bent,
Far off yet near—the goal of all desire.

So daily dying to the way of self,
So daily living to your way of love,
We walk the road, Lord Jesus, that you trod,
Knowing ourselves, baptized into your death:
So we are dead and live with you in God.

If dead in you, so in you we arise,
You the first-born of all the faithful dead;
And as through stoney ground the green
      shoots break,
Glorious in springtime dress of leaf and flower,
So in the Father's glory shall we wake. Amen.

Text: Thomas H. Cain (1931), © 1982; *Hymnal of the Hours* (Chicago: GIA Pub., 1989), #79.

Psalm 51   King David's Prayer for Forgiveness

Antiphon   If we die with the Lord, *
                   we shall live with the Lord.

Be merciful to me, O God,
because of your constant love.
Because of your great mercy
wipe away my sins!
Wash away all my evil
and make me clean from my sin!

I recognize my faults;
I am always conscious of my sins.
I have sinned against you—only against you—
and done what you consider evil.

So you are right in judging me;
you are justified in condemning me.

I have been evil from the day I was born;
from the time I was conceived, I have been sinful.

Sincerity and truth are what you require;
fill my mind with your wisdom.
Remove my sin, and I will be clean;
wash me, and I shall be whiter than snow.

Let me hear the sounds of joy and gladness;
and though you have crushed me and broken me,
I will be happy once again.
Close your eyes to my sins
and wipe out all my evil.

Create a pure heart in me, O God,
and put a new and loyal spirit in me.
Do not banish me from your presence;
Do not take your holy spirit away from me.

Give me again the joy that comes from
        your salvation,
and make me willing to obey you.
Then I will teach sinners your commands,
and they will turn back to you.

Spare my life, O God, and save me,
and I will gladly proclaim your righteousness.
Help me to speak, Lord,
and I will praise you.

You do not want sacrifices,
or I would offer them;
you are not pleased with burnt offerings.
My sacrifice is a humble spirit, O God;
you will not reject a humble and repentant heart.

Antiphon   If we die with the Lord,
               we shall live with the Lord.

Psalm Prayer

Gracious God, our Father,
when David repented in sackcloth and ashes
you poured out on him the healing medicine
of your forgiveness.
Help us to follow his example,
give us a humble and repentant heart
and pardon all our transgressions.
We ask this through Christ Jesus our Lord.
—Amen.

Reading   Matthew 5:1-11

Jesus saw the crowds and went up a hill, where he sat
down. His disciples gathered around him, and he began
to teach them:

Happy are those who know they are spiritually poor;
the Kingdom of heaven belongs to them!
Happy are those who mourn;

God will comfort them!
Happy are those who are humble;
they will receive what God has promised!
Happy are those whose greatest desire is to do what
God requires;
God will satisfy them fully!
Happy are those who are merciful to others;
God will be merciful to them!
Happy are the pure in heart;
they will see God!
Happy are those who work for peace;
God will call them his children!
Happy are those who are persecuted
because they do what God requires;
the Kingdom of heaven belongs to them!
Happy are you when people insult you and
persecute you
and tell all kinds of evil lies against you
because you are my followers.
Be happy and glad,
for a great reward is kept for you in heaven.
This is how the prophets who lived before you
were persecuted.

Response
Create a pure heart in me, O God,
—and put a new and loyal spirit in me.

Canticle of Ezekiel   36:24-28

Antiphon   When the Spirit comes, *
                he will lead you into all truth.

I will draw you from the nations,
gather you from exile
and bring you home.
I will wash you in fresh water,
rid you of the filth of idols
and make you clean again.

I will make you a new heart,
breathe new spirit into you.
I will remove your heart of stone,
give you back a heart of flesh.

I will give you my own Spirit
to lead you in my ways,
faithful to what I command.

Then you will live in the land,
the land I gave your ancestors.
You will be my people
and I will be your God.

Glory to the Father, and to the Son,
and to the Holy Spirit:
as it was in the beginning, is now,
and will be for ever. Amen.

Antiphon   When the Spirit comes,
             he will lead you into all truth.

Prayer

Show us your mercy, O Lord;
—and grant us your salvation.
Clothe your ministers with righteousness;
—let your people sing with joy.
Give peace, O Lord, in all the world;
—for only in you can we live in safety.
Lord, keep this nation under your care;
—and guide us in the way of justice and truth.
Let your way be known upon earth;
—your saving health among all nations.
Let not the needy, O Lord, be forgotten;
—nor the hope of the poor be taken away.
Create in us clean hearts, O God;
—and sustain us with your Holy Spirit.

Text: *Book of Common Prayer* (1979), pp. 97-98.

(spontaneous prayer)

Prayer

Lord Jesus Christ,
at first you came among us
as the suffering servant of God.
When you come again in glory
to judge the living and the dead,
be our peace and our salvation,
for you have redeemed us
with your precious blood.
You live and reign now and forever.
—Amen.

Blessing

May the God of mercy and compassion,
through the merits of Jesus,
+ deliver us from all evil.
—Amen.

*****

A Consideration

Consider well that both by night and day
While we most busily provide and care
For our disport, our revel, and our play,
For pleasant melody and dainty fare,
Death stealeth on full slily; unaware
He lieth at hand and shall us all surprise,
We know not when nor where nor in what wise.

When fierce temptations threat thy soul with loss
Think on his passion and the bitter pain,
Think on the mortal anguish of the cross,
Think on Christ's blood let out at every vein,
Think on his precious heart all rent in twain;
For thy redemption think all this was wrought,
Nor be that lost which he so dearly bought.

St. Thomas More, martyr (1478-1535)

*****

Evening Prayer

Jesus Christ + is the light of the world,
—a light no darkness can extinguish.

Hymn

O Christ, you are the light and day
Which drives away the night,
The ever shining Sun of God
And pledge of future light.

As now the evening shadows fall,
O grant us, Lord, we pray,
A quiet night to rest in you
Until the break of day.

Remember us, poor mortals all,
We humbly ask, O Lord,
And may your presence in our souls
Be now our great reward. Amen.

Text: *Christe, qui lux es*, ca. 800; trans. Frank Quinn, O.P., © 1989, GIA Inc.

Psalm 36b   The Goodness of God

Antiphon   We find protection * under the shadow
            of your cross.

Lord, your constant love reaches the heavens;
your faithfulness extends to the skies.
Your righteousness is towering like the mountains;
your justice is like the depths of the sea.
People and animals are in your care.

How precious, O God, is your constant love!
We find protection under the shadow of your wings.
We feast on the abundant food you provide;
you let us drink from the river of your goodness.
You are the source of all life,
and because of your light we see the light.

Continue to love those who know you
and to do good to those who are righteous.
Do not let proud people attack me
or the wicked make me run away.

Antiphon   We find protection under the shadow
            of your cross.

Psalm Prayer

Lord of life and light,
we rejoice in your constant love.
Protect us under the shadow of your cross

and make us walk in your light,
for you are our brother and our savior,
O Christ our Lord,
living and reigning forever and ever.
—Amen.

Reading   Isaiah 55:6-7

Turn to the Lord and pray to him, now that he is near. Let the wicked leave their way of life and change their way of thinking. Let them turn to the Lord, our God; he is merciful and quick to forgive.

Response

Close your eyes to my sins, O Lord,
—and wipe out all my evil.

Canticle of Mary   Luke 1:46-55

Antiphon   Blessed be the Lord * who has come to
             us and set us free.

My soul + proclaims the greatness of the Lord,
my spirit rejoices in God my Savior
for he has looked with favor on his lowly servant.

From this day all generations will call me blessed:
the Almighty has done great things for me,
and holy is his Name.

He has mercy on those who fear him
in every generation.

He has shown the strength of his arm,
he has scattered the proud in their conceit.

He has cast down the mighty from their thrones,
and has lifted up the lowly.

He has filled the hungry with good things,
and the rich he has sent away empty.

He has come to the help of his servant Israel
for he has remembered his promise of mercy,
the promise he made to our ancestors,
to Abraham and his children for ever.

Glory to the Father, and to the Son,
    and to the Holy Spirit:
as it was in the beginning, is now,
    and will be for ever. Amen.

Antiphon   Blessed be the Lord who has come to
            us and set us free.

Litany to Christ our Lord (pp. 288-291), or Litany of the Sacred Heart of Jesus (pp. 295-297) or this prayer

Lord Jesus Christ,
you loved us and delivered yourself up for us
as an agreeable and fragrant sacrifice to God;
rescue us from our former darkness
and teach us to walk as children of the light
in all goodness, justice, and truth.
You live and reign now and forever.
—Amen.

Blessing

May the blessing of almighty God,
+ the Father, the Son, and the Holy Spirit,
descend upon us and remain with us for ever.
—Amen.

Marian Anthem for Lent

Hail, Queen of Heaven, beyond compare,
to whom the angels homage pay;
hail, Root of Jesse, Gate of Light,
that opened for the world's new day.

Rejoice, O Virgin unsurpassed,
in whom our ransom was begun,
for all your loving children pray
to Christ, our Savior, and your Son.

Text: © 1974 *Stanbrook Abbey Hymnal*

Holy Week

In Honor of the Five Wounds of Christ Crucified

The cross is the center of Christian devotion. The body of the Savior on the cross—lacerated from the scourging, wounded by the helmet of thorns, and pierced hands and feet by nails—is the precious burden it presents to the eyes of faith. The wounds made by the nails and by the soldier's lance through his side are the ultimate signs of total giving for us and for our salvation.

This devotion to the Five Wounds is attributed to St. Clare of Assisi (1194-1253). She was not only the ardent disciple of Jesus crucified but also the closest follower of St. Francis of Assisi. It was he who spent the final years of his life actually transfixed by nails of flesh in his hands and feet and with a gaping wound in his side. As a living crucifix Francis inspired new devotion to the cross, the broken body and the five wounds of Christ.

This form of devotion to the Five Wounds is especially suitable for Holy Week, but may, of course, be used at any time.

In honor of the wound in the right hand:

Praise and glory to you, Lord Jesus,
for the holy wound in your right hand.
Through this wound of love
forgive all the sins I have committed
in thought, word, and deed,
by neglect of your service,
and by my self-indulgence,
both waking and sleeping.
Help me to keep your death on the cross
and your sacred wounds always before my mind.
I want to show my gratitude to you
by carrying my own cross each day for your sake.
Grant this, Lord Jesus,
you who live and reign forever and ever.
—Amen.

In honor of the wound in the left hand:

Praise and glory to you, Lord Jesus,
for the wound in your left hand.
Through this wound of love,
have mercy on me and remove from my heart
anything that displeases you.
Grant me victory over the relentless enemies
who wage war against me.

Fill me with your strength
so that I may trample on them all.
Through your merciful death
deliver me from all the dangers
that threaten my life and my salvation
and make me worthy of sharing
in your glorious kingdom,
where you live and reign forever and ever.
—Amen.

In honor of the wound in the right foot:

Praise and glory to you, Jesus, good Savior,
for the holy wound in your right foot.
Through this wound of love,
grant that I may truly repent
in proportion to the magnitude of my sins.
Through your death on the cross.
keep this community of ours
continually united to your will
and preserve it body and soul from all adversity.
When the dreadful day of judgment comes,
receive my soul into your mercy
and grant it eternal joy, O Lord,
you who live and reign forever and ever.
—Amen.

In honor of the wound in the left foot:

Praise and glory to you, merciful Jesus,
for the holy wound in your left foot.
Through this wound of love,
grant me full pardon of all my sins
so that before I die I may
confess all my sins with perfect contrition,
receive the sacrament of your body and blood,
be anointed for glory and pass on to you
in complete purity of body and mind.
Hear my prayer, O Lord,
you who live and reign forever and ever.
—Amen.

In honor of the wound in the side:

Praise and glory to you, Jesus, worthy of all love,
for the wound in your holy side.
Through this wound of love,
we see your immense mercy revealed,
not only to the Roman soldier who pierced
　　　　your heart,
but to us all.
I am now being delivered from every evil,
past, present, and yet to come,
through the merits of your precious blood

offered and received throughout the whole world.
By your bitter death,
grant me lively faith, unshakable hope
and perfect charity,
so that I may love you with all my heart
and mind and strength
and my neighbor as myself.
Establish me in your holy ways,
so that I may persevere in your service
and please you now and always.
—Amen

We adore you, O Christ, and we bless you,
—for by your holy cross you have redeemed
      the world.

Let us pray.

Almighty and eternal God,
you redeemed the human race
through the five wounds of your Son,
our Lord Jesus Christ.
As we worship these wounds of love,
rescue us from a sudden and eternal death
by the merits of his blood and his own dying.
We ask this through the same Lord Jesus,
who lives and reigns with you and the Holy Spirit
one God, for ever and ever.
—Amen.

Eastertide (50 Days)

Easter is the culmination of the gospel and of the liturgical year. In its light we can detect the full meaning of the person and ministry of Jesus, from Bethlehem to Golgotha and the empty tomb. God vindicated Jesus in raising him from the dead and sat him down at his right hand in heaven—and us with him! Like the wounds in his risen body, the divine sacraments of the Church are the visible signs of his continuing presence and power among us.

Morning Prayer

Christ + is risen, alleluia!
—He is risen indeed, alleluia!

Hymn

On Easter morn at break of day
the faithful women went their way
to see the tomb where Jesus lay, alleluia!

An angel clad in white they see,
who sat and spoke unto the three:
"Your Lord has gone to Galilee!" alleluia!

That night the apostles met in fear,
when Christ did in their midst appear,
and said: "My peace be with you here!" alleluia!

Text: Jean Tisserand (d. 1494), trans. John Mason Neale (1818-1866), alt.

Psalm 47   The Resurrection and Ascension

Antiphon   Christ ascended * to fill the whole
           universe with his presence, alleluia!

Clap your hands for joy, all peoples!
Praise God with loud songs!
The Lord, the Most High, is to be feared;
he is a great king, ruling over all the world.
He gave us victory over the peoples;
he made us rule over the nations.
He chose for us the land where we live,
the proud possession of his people, whom he loves.

God goes up to his throne.
There are shouts of joy and the blast of trumpets,
as the Lord goes up.
Sing praise to God;
sing praise to our king.
God is king over all the world;
praise him with songs!

God sits on his sacred throne;
he rules over the nations.
The rulers of the nations assemble
with the people of the God of Abraham.
More powerful than all armies is he;
he rules supreme.

Antiphon   Christ ascended to fill the whole
             universe with his presence, alleluia!

Psalm Prayer

Almighty and everlasting God,
grant that we who believe
that your only-begotten Son, our Savior,
rose from the dead and ascended into heaven,
may ourselves dwell in spirit amid heavenly things;
through the same Christ our Lord.
—Amen.

Reading   1 Peter 1:3-5

Let us give thanks to the God and Father of our Lord
Jesus Christ! Because of his great mercy he gave us new
life by raising Jesus Christ from death. This fills us with
a living hope, and so we look forward to possessing the
rich blessings that God keeps for his people. He keeps
them for you in heaven, where they cannot decay or spoil
or fade away. They are for you, who through faith are

kept safe by God's power for the salvation which is ready
to be revealed at the end of time.

Response

Thanks be to God who gives the victory, alleluia!
—Through our Lord Jesus Christ, alleluia!

Te Deum Laudamus

You are God: we praise you;
You are the Lord: we acclaim you;
You are the eternal Father:
All creation worships you.

To you all angels, all the powers of heaven,
Cherubim and Seraphim, sing in endless praise:
Holy, holy, holy Lord, God of power and might,
heaven and earth are full of your glory.

The glorious company of apostles praise you.
The noble fellowship of prophets praise you.
The white-robed army of martyrs praise you.

Throughout the world the holy Church
acclaims you:
Father of majesty unbounded,
your true and only Son, worthy of all worship,
and the Holy Spirit, advocate and guide.

You, Christ, are the king of glory,
the eternal Son of the Father.

When you became man to set us free
you did not spurn the Virgin's womb.

You overcame the sting of death
and opened the kingdom of heaven to all believers.

You are seated at God's right hand in glory.
We believe that you will come and be our judge.

Come, then, Lord, and help your people,
bought with the price of your own blood,
and bring us with your saints
to glory everlasting.

Prayers

Lord Jesus, who died for our sins and rose for
        our salvation,
—hear us, risen Lord.
Lord Jesus, who trampled down death by your death,
—hear us, risen Lord.
Lord Jesus, who brought life to those in the grave,
—hear us, risen Lord.
Lord Jesus, who gave fresh life to a fallen world,
—hear us, risen Lord.

Lord Jesus, our life and our resurrection,
—hear us, risen Lord.

(spontaneous prayer)

Prayer

Only-begotten Son and eternal Word of God,
for us and for our salvation,
you took flesh of the Virgin Mary
and came to live among us as a man.
For our sake you were crucified,
mastered death and the grave,
and rose again on the third day.
Forgive us our sins
and sanctify us to your service,
for you are the joy of those who love you,
O Savior of the world,
living and reigning with the Father and the
        Holy Spirit,
now and for ever.
—Amen.

Let us bless the Lord, alleluia!
—Thanks be to God, alleluia!

*****

Christ Is Risen

Away with the pleading of poverty:
the kingdom belongs to us all.
Away with the bewailing of failings:
forgiveness has come from the grave.
Away with your fears of dying:
the death of our Savior has freed us from fear.
Death played the master:
he has mastered death.
The world below had scarcely known him
      in the flesh
when he rose and left it plunged in bitter mourning.

Isaiah knew it would be so.
The world of shadows mourned, he cried,
      when it met you,
mourned at its bringing low, wept at its deluding.

The shadows seized a body and found it was God;
they reached for earth and what they held
      was heaven;
they took what they could see: it was what no
      one sees.
Where is death's goad? Where is the shadows'
      victory?

Christ is risen: the world below is in ruins.
Christ is risen: the spirits of evil are fallen.
Christ is risen: the angels of God are rejoicing.
Christ is risen: the tombs are void of their dead.
Christ has indeed arisen from the dead,
    the first of the sleepers.

Glory and power are his for ever and ever. Amen.

Text: St. Hippolytus of Rome, bishop and martyr (ca. 165-235), trans. from the Greek by Walter Mitchell: Robert Atwan et al. (eds.), *Divine Inspiration* (New York: Oxford Univ. Press, 1998) p. 264.

*****

Evening Prayer
Christ + is risen, alleluia!
—He is risen indeed, alleluia!

Hymn Based on Isaiah 63:1-7
Who is this who comes in triumph,
Clothed in royal garments dyed with blood,
Walking in the greatness of his glory,
Bearing in his hand the holy rood?

This is Christ the risen Lord, the Strong One,
He who trod the winepress all alone;

Out of death he comes with life unending,
Seeking those he purchased for his own.

Great and wonderful is our Redeemer,
Christ the Living One, the just and true,
Praise him with the Father and the Spirit,
Ever with us, making all things new.

Text: © 1974 *Stanbrook Abbey Hymnal*

Easter Anthem   Christ Our Passover

Christ our Passover has been sacrificed for us;
therefore let us keep the feast,
not with the old leaven, the leaven of
          malice and evil,
but with the unleavened bread of sincerity and
          truth. Alleluia!

Christ, being raised from the dead, will never
          die again;
death no longer has dominion over him.
The death that he died, he died to sin, once for all;
but the life he lives, he lives to God.
So also consider yourselves dead to sin,
and alive to God in Jesus Christ our Lord. Alleluia!

Christ has been raised from the dead,
the first fruits of those who have fallen asleep.
For since by a man came death,
by a man has come also the resurrection of the dead.
For as in Adam all die,
so also in Christ shall all be made alive. Alleluia!

Text: 1 Corinthians 5:7-8; Romans 6:9-11; 1 Corinthians. 15:20-22: *Book of Common Prayer* (1979), p. 83.

Prayer

Almighty and ever-living God,
you sealed a covenant of reconciliation with us
in the mystery of Christ's passing through death
      to life.
May we come to everlasting joy
by a holy keeping of these Easter festivities.
We ask this through Christ our risen Lord.
—Amen.

Reading   1 Peter 1:13-16

Keep alert and set your hope completely on the blessing which will be given you when Jesus Christ is revealed. Be obedient to God, and do not allow your lives to be shaped by those desires you had when you were still ignorant. Instead, be holy in all that you do, just as God who called you is holy. The Scripture says, "Be holy because I am holy."

Response

Just as Christ was raised from death, alleluia!
—We also must live a new life, alleluia!

Canticle of Mary   Luke 1:46-55

Antiphon   Joy fill your heart, O Queen most high,
            alleluia! *
            your Son who in the tomb did lie,
            alleluia!
            Has risen as he did prophesy, alleluia!
            Pray for us, Mother, when we die,
            alleluia!

Text: Trans. James Quinn, S.J., *Praise for All Seasons*, p. 97.

My soul + proclaims the greatness of the Lord,
my spirit rejoices in God my Savior;
for he has looked with favor on his lowly servant.

From this day all generations will call me blessed:
the Almighty has done great things for me,
and holy is his Name.

He has mercy on those who fear him
in every generation.

He has shown the strength of his arm,
he has scattered the proud in their conceit.

He has cast down the mighty from their thrones,
and has lifted up the lowly.

He has filled the hungry with good things,
and the rich he has sent away empty.

He has come to the help of his servant Israel
for he has remembered his promise of mercy,
the promise he made to our ancestors,
to Abraham and his children for ever.

Glory to the Father, and to the Son,
and to the Holy Spirit:
as it was in the beginning, is now,
and will be for ever. Amen.

The above antiphon is repeated.

The Victorious Cross

We adore you, Lord Jesus Christ,
as you ascend your cross.
—May this cross deliver us from the
destroying angel.

We adore your wounded body
as it hangs on the cross.
—May your wounds be our healing.
We adore you dead and buried in the tomb.
—May your death be our life.
We adore you as you descend among the dead to
       deliver them.
—May we never hear the dread sentence of doom.
We adore you rising from the dead.
—Free us from the weight of our sins.
We adore you ascending to the right hand of God.
—Raise us with all your saints to eternal glory.
We adore you as you come to judge the living and
       the dead.
—At this coming be not our judge but our Savior.
Holy God, holy Mighty One, holy Immortal One,
—Have mercy on us.

Text: From a tenth century Latin manuscript.

(spontaneous prayer)

Prayer

Lord Jesus Christ,
by your cross and resurrection
you have mastered death
and brought life to those in the grave.
May your blessed passion

be the joy of the whole world
and may your glorious rising from the tomb
ever be our song,
O Savior of the world,
living and reigning with the Father
and the Holy Spirit,
now and for ever.
—Amen.

Blessing

Let us bless the Lord, alleluia!
—Thanks be to God, alleluia!
May the risen Christ,
the Lord of life and death,
+ bless us and keep us.
—Amen.

Pentecost and the Church

The long season after Pentecost Sunday, the close of the Easter season, is termed Ordinary Time. It calls upon us to recognize that we live in the time of the Church while we wait for the full coming of the reign of God. With all its divine radiance and its Spirit-filled sacraments, the church needs to pray and work to explore, understand, and live out the gospel. Jesus' final and most charged gift was the Holy Spirit that fell upon Mary and the Apostles on Pentecost. The Spirit lives on in the church, teaching, urging, counseling and fortifying us. The single form of prayer offered here is suitable for either morning or evening.

Come, Holy Spirit, fill the hearts of your faithful,
—And kindle in them the fire of your divine love.

Veni, Creator Spiritus

Creator spirit, by whose aid
The world's foundations first were laid,
Come visit every pious mind;
Come pour thy joys on humankind;
From sin and sorrow set us free,
And make thy temples worthy thee.

O source of uncreated light,
The Father's promised Paraclete!
Thrice holy fount, thrice holy fire,
Our hearts with heavenly love inspire;
Come, and thy sacred unction bring
To sanctify us, while we sing.

Plenteous of grace, descend from high,
Rich in thy sevenfold energy!
Thou strength of his Almighty hand
Whose power does heaven and earth command.
Proceeding Spirit, our defense,
Who do'st the gifts of tongues dispense,
And crown'st thy gifts with eloquence.

Refine and purge our earthly parts;
But, O, inflame and fire our hearts!
Our frailties help, our vice control,
Submit the senses to the soul;
And, when rebellious they are grown,
Then lay thy hand, and hold them down.

Chase from our minds, the infernal foes;
And peace, the fruit of love, bestow:
And, lest our feet should step astray,
Protect and guide us in the way.

Make us eternal truths receive,
And practice all that we believe;
Give us thyself, that we may see
The Father, and the Son, by thee.

Immortal hour, endless fame,
Attend the Almighty Father's name;
The Savior Son be glorified,
Who for lost man's redemption died;
And equal adoration be,
Eternal Paraclete to thee.

Text: John Dryden (1631-1700).

Psalm 104　God, Creator and Provider

Antiphon　　Tongues of fire * touched each
person there.

I will bless you, Lord my God!
You fill the world with awe.
You dress yourself in light,
in rich, majestic light.

You stretched the sky like a tent,
built your house beyond the rain.
You ride upon the clouds,

the wind becomes your wings,
the storm becomes your herald,
your servants bolts of light.

You drench the hills
with rain from high heaven.
You nourish the earth
with what your create.

You make grass grow for cattle,
make plants grow for people,
food to eat from the earth
and wine to warm the heart,
oil to glisten on faces
and bread for bodily strength.

God, how fertile your genius!
You shape each thing,
you fill the world
with what you do.

All look to you for food
when they hunger;
you provide it and they feed.
You open your hand, they feast;
you turn away, they fear.

You steal their breath,
they drop back into dust.
Breathe into them, they rise;
the face of the earth comes alive!

Let God's glory endure
and the Lord delight in creating.
I will sing to my God,
make music for the Lord
as long as I live.

Antiphon   Tongues of fire touched each
person there

Psalm Prayer

Creator and Preserver of the universe,
you continually renew our lives
by fresh outpourings of the Holy Spirit,
our advocate and guide.
We thank you for all your gifts
and look to you for every blessing
so that we may be perfect in your sight.
We ask this through Christ our Lord.
—Amen.

Reading   Acts 2:41-47

Many of them believed Peter's message and were baptized, and about three thousand people were added to the group that day. They spent their time in learning from the apostles, taking part in the fellowship, and sharing in the fellowship of meals and prayers. Many miracles and wonders were being done through the apostles, and everyone was filled with awe. All the believers continued together in close fellowship and shared their belongings with one another. They would sell their property and possessions, and distribute the money among all, according to what each one needed. Day after day they met as a group in the Temple, and they had their meals together in their homes, eating with glad and humble hearts, praising God, and enjoying the good will of all the people. And every day the Lord added to their group those who were being saved.

Response

Whoever calls out to the Lord for help, alleluia!
—Will be saved, alleluia!

Litany to the Holy Spirit
(or see another litany on p. 286)

Lord and life-giving Spirit,
    you brooded over the primeval waters.
—Come, fill our hearts.

You led your people out of slavery in Egypt
   and into the freedom of the promised land.
—Come, fill our hearts.
You overshadowed Mary of Nazareth
   and made her the Mother of God.
—Come, fill our hearts.
You anointed Jesus as Messiah
   when he was baptized by John in the Jordan.
—Come, fill our hearts.
You raised Jesus out of death
   and proclaimed him Son of God in all his power.
—Come, fill our hearts.
You appeared on Pentecost in tongues of flame
   and endowed your Church with charismatic gifts.
—Come, fill our hearts.
You send us out to testify to the Good News
   about Jesus Christ.
—Come, fill our hearts.

(spontaneous prayer)

Prayer

Holy Spirit of truth,
Sovereign Lord of the universe,
guide and guardian of your people,
present everywhere,
overflowing all that exists:

Come and dwell in us,
cleanse us from all sin,
pour out your blessings on us,
give us fresh life,
and in your gracious love
bring us to salvation.
—Amen.

or this prayer

God of fire and light,
on the first Pentecost,
you formed the hearts
of those who believed in you
by the indwelling of the Holy Spirit:
Under the inspiration of that same Spirit
give us a taste for what is right and true
and a continuing sense
of his joy-bringing presence and power;
through Christ Jesus our Lord.
—Amen.

Blessing

May the grace of our Lord Jesus Christ
+ and the love of God
and the fellowship of the Holy Spirit
be with us all for ever.
—Amen.

A Marian Anthem Throughout the Year

Hail, our Queen and Mother blest!
joy when all was sadness,
life and hope you brought to earth,
mother of our gladness.
Children of the sinful Eve,
sinless Eve, befriend us,
exiled in this vale of tears:
strength and comfort send us!

Pray for us, O Patroness,
be our consolation!
Lead us home to see your Son,
Jesus, our salvation!
Gracious are you, full of grace,
loving as none other,
joy of heaven and joy of earth,
Mary, God's own Mother!

Text: *Salve Regina,* eleventh century, trans. James Quinn, S.J.,
Praise for All Seasons, p. 96.

All seasons are fruitful for Christians,
for all are full of Jesus Christ.

Bishop Jacques Bossuet (1627-1704)

5. Night Prayer

As each day draws to a close, we commend ourselves into the hands of our heavenly Father. God freely forgives us our daily faults, refreshes us with sleep, and conducts us safely through the night to another day of love and service. This form of Compline may be used to close church meetings or other occasions that finish late in the evening.

When Night Prayer is prayed with others, the stanzas of the psalms, the hymn and the Song of Simeon may be alternated between the leader and the group or the group may divide in two and alternate the stanzas in that fashion. The antiphons are recited by all before and after the psalm and the Song of Simeon.

Confession

Leader: Our help + is in the name of the Lord,
All: —the maker of heaven and earth.

Leader: Let us confess our sins to God and to
one another.
(brief examination of conscience)
All: —I confess to Almighty God
and to you, my brothers and sisters,
that I have sinned through my own fault
in my thoughts and in my words,
in what I have done,
and in what I have failed to do;
and I ask blessed Mary, ever virgin,
all the angels and saints,
and you, my brothers and sisters,
to pray for me to the Lord our God.

Leader: May almighty God have mercy on us,
+ forgive us our sins,
and bring us to everlasting life.
All: —Amen.

Hymn

> Lord Jesus Christ, abide with us,
> now that the sun has run its course;
> let hope not be obscured by night
> but may faith's darkness be as light.
>
> Lord Jesus Christ, grant us your peace,
> and when the trials of earth shall cease,
> grant us the morning light of grace,
> the radiant splendor of your face.
>
> Immortal, Holy, Threefold Light,
> yours be the kingdom, power and might;
> all glory be eternally
> to you, life-giving Trinity! Amen.

Text: *Mane nobiscum, Domine*, para. St Joseph Abbey, © 1968.

Psalmody

> Pray one or more of the following three psalms and the psalm prayer and then turn to page 285.

Psalm 4   Trust in God's Care

> Antiphon   Be kind to me now, O Lord, * and hear my prayer.

273

Answer me when I pray,
O God, my defender!
When I was in trouble, you helped me.
Be kind to me now and hear my prayer.

How long will you people insult me?
How long will you love what is worthless
and go after what is false?

Remember that the Lord has chosen
the righteous for his own,
and he hears me when I call to him.

Tremble with fear and stop sinning;
think deeply about this,
when you lie in silence on your beds.
Offer the right sacrifices to the Lord,
and put your trust in him.

There are many who pray:
"Give us more blessings, O Lord.
Look on us with kindness!"
But the joy that you have given me
is more than they will ever have
with all their grain and wine.

When I lie down, I go to sleep in peace;
you alone, O Lord, keep me perfectly safe.

Glory to the Father, and to the Son,
and to the Holy Spirit:
as it was in the beginning, is now,
and will be for ever. Amen.

Antiphon   Be kind to me now, O Lord, and hear
              my prayer.

Psalm Prayer

Leader: Let us pray (pause for silent prayer).
         You consoled your Son in his anguish
         and released him from the darkness of the grave.
         Lord, turn your face toward us
         that we may sleep in your peace
         and rise in your light.
         We ask this through Christ our Lord.
All: —Amen.

Psalm 91   God's Sheltering Care

Antiphon   I have given you the power *
              to tread upon serpents and scorpions.

Whoever goes to the Lord for safety,
whoever remains under the protection of the
    Almighty,

can say to him, "You are my defender and protector.
You are my God; in you I trust."

He will keep you safe from all hidden dangers
and from all deadly diseases.
He will cover you with his wings;
you will be safe in his care;
his faithfulness will protect and defend you.

You need not fear any dangers at night
or sudden attacks during the day
or the plagues that strike in the dark
or the evils that kill in daylight.

A thousand may fall dead beside you,
ten thousand all around you,
but you will not be harmed.
You will look and see
how the wicked are punished.

You have made the Lord your defender,
the Most High your protector,
and so no disaster will strike you,
no violence will come near your home.
God will put his angels in charge of you
to protect you wherever you go.
They will hold you up with their hands

to keep you from hurting your feet on the stones.
You will trample down lions and snakes,
fierce lions and poisonous snakes.

God says, "I will save those who love me
and will protect those who know me as Lord.
When they call to me, I will answer them;
when they are in trouble, I will be with them.
I will rescue them and honor them.
I will reward them with long life;
I will save them."

Glory to the Father, and to the Son,
and to the Holy Spirit:
as it was in the beginning, is now,
and will be for ever. Amen.

Antiphon   I have given you the power
                 to tread upon serpents and scorpions.

Psalm Prayer

Leader: Let us pray (pause for silent prayer).
Lord Jesus Christ,
when tempted by the devil,
you remained loyal to your Father
whose angels watched over you at his command.
Guard your Church and keep us from the
plague of sin
so that we may remain loyal
to the day we enjoy your salvation and glory.
You live and reign for ever and ever.

All: —Amen.

Psalm 134   We Praise God Through the Night

Antiphon   Praise God, * all you his servants, small
and great.

Come, praise the Lord, all his servants,
all who serve in his Temple at night.
Raise your hands in prayer in the Temple,
and praise the Lord!

May the Lord, who made heaven and earth,
bless you from Zion!

Glory to the Father, and to the Son,
and to the Holy Spirit:
as it was in the beginning, is now,
and will be for ever. Amen.

Antiphon   Praise God, all you his servants, small
            and great.

Psalm Prayer

Leader: Let us pray (pause for silent prayer).

All your servants praise and thank you, Lord.
Be our light as night descends.
We lift up to you the good works of our hands;
grant us your generous blessing.
We ask this through Christ our Lord.

All: —Amen.

Reading

One of the following scripture passages is now read.

Remember this! The Lord—and the Lord alone—is
our God. Love the Lord your God with all your heart,
with all your soul, and with all your strength. Never forget these commands that I am giving you today. Teach
them to your children. Repeat them when you are at

home and when you are away, when you are resting and when you are working (Deuteronomy 6:4-7).

All: Thanks be to God.

Sisters and brothers: Be alert, be on the watch! Your enemy, the Devil, roams around like a roaring lion, looking for someone to devour. Be firm in your faith and resist him (1 Peter 5:8-9).

All: Thanks be to God.

Surely, Lord, you are with us! We are your people; do not abandon us (Jeremiah 14:9).

All: Thanks be to God.

Response

Into your hands, O Lord, I commend my spirit.
—Into your hands, O Lord, I commend my spirit.
You have redeemed us, Lord God of Truth.
—I commend my spirit.
Glory to the Father, and to the Son, and to the
  Holy Spirit.
—Into your hands, O Lord, I commend my spirit.

Song of Simeon   Luke 2:29

> Antiphon   Guard us, O Lord, while we are awake *
>   and keep us while we sleep,
>   that waking we may watch with Christ
>   and sleeping we may rest in peace.

Lord, + now let your servant go in peace;
your word has been fulfilled:

my own eyes have seen the salvation
which you have prepared in the sight of every people:

a light to reveal you to the nations
and the glory of your people Israel.

Glory to the Father, and to the Son,
and to the Holy Spirit:

as it was in the beginning, is now,
and will be for ever. Amen.

The above antiphon is repeated.

Prayer

Leader: Lighten our darkness, O Lord,
and by your great mercy
defend us from all perils and dangers
of this coming night;
for the love of your only Son, our Savior
Jesus Christ.

All: —Amen.

Conclusion

Leader: May all who have died in Christ rest in
his peace.

All: —Amen.

Leader: May the Lord give + us a peaceful night as
day's perfect ending.

All: —Amen.

The Marian anthem "Hail, our Queen" (*Salve Regina*) may be used to conclude Night Prayer (see p. 374).

6. Litanies

Our Lord not only taught us to pray, but he commanded us to pray: insistently, perseveringly, without ceasing (Matthew 7:7-11; Mark 11:20-25; Luke 11:1-22; 18:1-8). In Christian devotion, one of the ways of persisting in prayer is through the use of litanies which invoke God, Christ, the Blessed Virgin, St. Joseph and other saints under a variety of titles and ascriptions of honor. These devotional litanies enjoy widespread usage among Catholic Christians, both as separate exercises of devotion and as part of morning and evening prayer.

The sacred triduum of Holy Week and the nine days of prayer that intervene between Ascension Thursday and Pentecost Sunday have suggested to Christians—particularly in time of special need—the practice of a three-day or a nine-day period of insistent prayer. Those who make such tridua or novenas often use one of the following litanies as a form of supplication.

The Divine Praises

Blessed be God.

Blessed be his holy name.

Blessed be Jesus Christ, true God and true man.

Blessed be the name of Jesus.

Blessed be his most sacred heart.

Blessed be his most precious blood.

Blessed be Jesus in the most holy sacrament of
the altar.

Blessed be the Holy Spirit, the Paraclete.

Blessed be the great Mother of God, Mary
most holy.

Blessed be her holy and immaculate conception.

Blessed be her glorious assumption.

Blessed be the name of Mary, virgin and mother.

Blessed be Saint Joseph, her most chaste spouse.

Blessed be God in his angels and in his saints.

Litany of the Holy Trinity

I

Father of Christ our Savior:

God of all consolation:

King of eternal ages:

King of the saints and angels:

Father of love and mercy:

Giver of every blessing:

—Stretch out your hand in healing.
Save us and make us one.

II
Jesus, eternal Wisdom:
Jesus, the joy of angels:
Jesus, the Son of Mary:
Jesus, our king and shepherd:
Jesus, our priest and victim:
Jesus, our hope of glory:

—Send us your Holy Spirit,
giver of joy and peace.

III
God the all-Holy Spirit:
Bond between Son and Father:
Gift of the new creation:
Fountain of life and goodness:
Seal on God's chosen children:
Peace of the Lord's own giving:

—Lead us through grace to glory,
one with the risen Christ.

Text: James Quinn, S.J.

Doxology

> To God the Father,
> who loved us and made us accepted
> in the Beloved:
> To God the Son, who loved us
> and loosed from our sins
> by his own blood:
> To God the Holy Spirit,
> who sheds the love of God
> abroad in our hearts:
> To the one true God,
> be all love and all glory for time and for eternity.
> —Amen.

Bishop Thomas Ken (1631-1711)

Litany to Christ Our Lord

Jesus says:
I am the bread of life.
I am the bread that came down from heaven.
If anyone eats this bread, he will live for ever
      (John 6:35, 41, 51).
—Lord, give us this bread always (John 6:34).

Jesus says:
I am the vine,
and you are the branches.
Whoever remains in me will bear much fruit,

for you can do nothing without me (John 15:5).
—Lord, we believe you are the Holy One
who has come from God (John 6:69).

Jesus says:
I am the gate.
Whoever comes in by me will be saved (John 10:9).
—Lord, Lord! Let us in! (Matthew 25:11).

Jesus says:
I am the light of the world.
Whoever follows me will have the light of life
and will never walk in darkness (John 8:12).
—Send us your light and your truth (Psalm 43:3).

Jesus says:
I am the good shepherd.
I know my sheep and they know me.
And I am willing to die for them (John 10:14-15).
—Lord, make us one flock with one shepherd
        (John 10:16).

Jesus says:
I am the resurrection and the life.
Whoever lives and believes in me will never die
        (John 11:25-26).
—Lord, I do believe that you are the Messiah,
        the Son of God (John 11:25).

Jesus says:
I am the way, the truth, and the life;
no one goes to the Father except by me (John 14:6).
—Teach me your ways, O Lord (Psalm 25:4).

Jesus says:
I am the one who knows everyone's thoughts
      and wishes.
I will repay each one of you according to what he
      has done (Revelation 2:22).
—Examine me, O God, and know my heart
      (Psalm 139:27).

Jesus says:
I am descended from the family of David.
I am the bright and the morning star
      (Revelation 22:16).
—Son of David, have mercy on me!
      (Matthew 15:22).

Jesus says:
I am the Alpha and the Omega,
the beginning and the end, the first and the last
      (Revelation 22:13).
—Lord, you show us that the first shall be last
and the last first (Matthew 19:30).

Prayer

Lord Jesus Christ,
the world's true sun,
ever rising, never setting,
whose life-giving warmth
engenders, preserves,
nourishes and gladdens
all things in heaven and on earth:
Shine in my soul, I pray,
scatter the night of sin,
and the clouds of error.

Blaze within me,
that I may go my way without stumbling,
taking no part in the shameful deeds
of those who wander in the dark,
but all my life long
walking as one native to the light.
—Amen.

Text: Desiderius Erasmus (1467-1536)

Litany of the Holy Name of Jesus

Lord, have mercy. —Lord, have mercy.
Christ, have mercy. —Christ, have mercy.
Lord, have mercy. —Lord have mercy.

God our Father in heaven, —Have mercy on us.
God the Son, Redeemer of the world,
  —Have mercy on us.
God the Holy Spirit, —Have mercy on us.
Holy Trinity, one God, —Have mercy on us.

Jesus, Son of the living God, —Have mercy on us.
Jesus, splendor of the Father,
Jesus, brightness of everlasting light,
Jesus, king of glory,
Jesus, dawn of justice,
Jesus, Son of the Virgin Mary,
Jesus, worthy of our love,
Jesus, worthy of our wonder,
Jesus, mighty God,
Jesus, father of the world to come,
Jesus, prince of peace,
Jesus, all-powerful,
Jesus, pattern of patience,
Jesus, model of obedience,
Jesus, gentle and humble of heart,

Jesus, lover of chastity,
Jesus, lover of us all,
Jesus, God of peace,

Jesus, author of life,
Jesus, model of goodness,
Jesus, seeker of souls,
Jesus, our God,
Jesus, our refuge,
Jesus, father of the poor,
Jesus, treasure of the faithful,

Jesus, good shepherd,
Jesus, true light,
Jesus, eternal wisdom,
Jesus, infinite goodness,
Jesus, our way and our life,
Jesus, joy of angels,
Jesus, king of patriarchs,
Jesus, teacher of apostles,
Jesus, master of evangelists,
Jesus, courage of martyrs,
Jesus, light of confessors,
Jesus, purity of virgins,
Jesus, crown of all saints,

Lord, be merciful,   —Jesus, save your people.
From all evil,
From every sin,
From the snares of the devil,
From your anger,
From the spirit of infidelity,

From everlasting death,
From neglect of your Holy Spirit,

By the mystery of your incarnation,
                    —Jesus, save your people.
By your birth,
By your childhood,
By your hidden life,
By your public ministry,
By your agony and crucifixion,
By your abandonment,
By your grief and sorrow,
By your death and burial,
By your rising to new life,
By your return in glory to the Father,
By your gift of the holy eucharist,
By your joy and glory,

Christ, hear us.   —Christ, hear us.
Lord Jesus, hear our prayer.
                    —Lord Jesus, hear our prayer.

Lamb of God, you take away the sins of the world,
                    —Have mercy on us.
Lamb of God, you take away the sins of the world,
                    —Have mercy on us.
Lamb of God, you take away the sins of the world,
                    —Have mercy on us.

Let us pray.

Lord, may we who honor the holy name of Jesus
enjoy his friendship in this life
and be filled with eternal joy in the kingdom
where he lives and reigns for ever and ever.
—Amen.

Note: In its present form this litany was approved for general use by Pope
Leo XIII (1878-1903).

Litany of the Sacred Heart of Jesus

Lord, have mercy.	—Lord, have mercy.
Christ, have mercy.	—Christ, have mercy.
Lord, have mercy.	—Lord, have mercy.

God our Father in heaven,   —Have mercy on us.
God the Son, Redeemer of the world,
                              —Have mercy on us.
God the Holy Spirit,   —Have mercy on us.
Holy Trinity, one God,   —Have mercy on us.

Heart of Jesus, Son of   —Have mercy on us.
    the eternal Father,
Heart of Jesus, formed by the Holy Spirit
    in the womb of the Virgin Mother,
Heart of Jesus, one with the eternal Word,
Heart of Jesus, infinite in majesty,
Heart of Jesus, holy temple of God,

Heart of Jesus, tabernacle of the Most High,
Heart of Jesus, house of God and gate of heaven,
Heart of Jesus, aflame with love for us,
Heart of Jesus, source of justice and love,
Heart of Jesus, full of goodness and love,
Heart of Jesus, well-spring of all virtue,
Heart of Jesus, worthy of all praise,
Heart of Jesus, king and center of all hearts,
Heart of Jesus, treasure-house of wisdom
        and knowledge,
Heart of Jesus, in whom there dwells the fullness
        of God,
Heart of Jesus, in whom the Father is well pleased,
Heart of Jesus, of whose fullness we have
        all received,
Heart of Jesus, desire of the eternal hills,
Heart of Jesus, patient and full of mercy,
Heart of Jesus, generous to all who turn to you,
Heart of Jesus, fountain of life and holiness,
Heart of Jesus, atonement for our sins,
Heart of Jesus, overwhelmed with insults,
Heart of Jesus, broken for our sins,
Heart of Jesus, obedient even to death,
Heart of Jesus, pierced by a lance,
Heart of Jesus, source of all consolation,
Heart of Jesus, our life and resurrection,
Heart of Jesus, our peace and reconciliation,

Heart of Jesus, victim for our sins,
Heart of Jesus, salvation of all who trust in you,
Heart of Jesus, hope of all who die in you,
Heart of Jesus, delight of all the saints,

Lamb of God, you take away the sins of the world,
—Have mercy on us.
Lamb of God, you take away the sins of the world,
—Have mercy on us.
Lamb of God, you take away the sins of the world,
—Have mercy on us.

Jesus, gentle and humble of heart,
—Touch our hearts and make them like your own.

Let us pray.

Father,
we rejoice in the gifts of love
we have received from the heart of Jesus your Son.
Open our hearts to share his life
and continue to bless us with his love.
We ask this in the name of Jesus the Lord.
—Amen.

Note: This litany was approved for general use by Pope Leo XIII (1878-1903).

Litany of the Blessed Sacrament of the Altar

Lord, have mercy.   —Lord, have mercy.

Christ, have mercy.   —Christ, have mercy.

Lord, have mercy.   —Lord, have mercy.

God our Father in heaven,   —Have mercy on us.

God the Son, Redeemer of the world,

                —Have mercy on us.

God the Holy Spirit,   —Have mercy on us.

Holy Trinity, one God,   —Have mercy on us.

Word made flesh and living among us,

                —Christ, have mercy on us.

Pure and acceptable sacrifice,

Hidden manna from above,

Living bread that came down from heaven,

Bread of life for a hungry world,

Chalice of blessing,

Precious blood that washes away our sins,

Memorial of God's undying love,

Food that lasts for eternal life,

Mystery of faith,

Medicine of immortality,

Food of God's chosen,

Perpetual presence in our tabernacles,

Viaticum of those who die in the Lord,

Pledge of future glory,
Be merciful,   —Spare us, Good Lord.
Be merciful,   —Graciously hear us, Good Lord.

By the great longing you had to eat the Passover with
     your disciples,

                         —Good Lord, deliver us.
By your humility in washing their feet,
By your loving gift of this divine sacrament,
By the five wounds of your precious body,
By your sacrificial death on the cross,
By the piercing of your sacred heart,
By your rising to new life,
By your gift of the Paraclete Spirit,
By your return in glory to judge the living and the dead,

Lamb of God, you take away the sins of the world,
                    —Have mercy on us.
Lamb of God, you take away the sins of the world,
                    —Have mercy on us.
Lamb of God, you take away the sins of the world,
                    —Have mercy on us.

You gave them bread from heaven to be their food.
           —And this bread contained all goodness.

Let us pray.

Lord Jesus Christ,
you gave us the Eucharist
as the memorial of your suffering and death.
May our worship of this sacrament of your body
and blood
help us to experience the salvation you won for us
and the peace of your kingdom,
where you live with the Father and the Holy Spirit,
one God for ever and ever.
—Amen.

Litany to the Spirit of the Seven Gifts

Come, Spirit of wisdom, and teach us to value the
highest gift.
—Come, Holy Spirit.
Come, Spirit of understanding, and show us all
things in the light of eternity.
—Come, Holy Spirit.
Come, Spirit of counsel, and guide us along the
straight and narrow path to our heavenly home.
—Come, Holy Spirit.
Come, Spirit of might, and strengthen us against
every evil spirit and interest which would
separate us from you.
—Come, Holy Spirit.
Come, Spirit of knowledge, and teach us the
shortness of life and the length of eternity.
—Come, Holy Spirit.

Come Spirit of godliness, and stir up our minds and
   hearts to love and serve the Lord our God
   all our days.
—Come, Holy Spirit.
Come, Spirit of the fear of the Lord, and make us
   tremble with awe and reverence before your
   divine majesty.
—Come, Holy Spirit.

Send forth your spirit and they shall be created.
—And you shall renew the face of the earth.

Let us pray.

Lord,
by the light of the Holy Spirit,
you have taught the hearts of your faithful.
In the same Spirit
help us to relish what is right
and always rejoice in your consolation.
We ask this through Christ our Lord.
—Amen.

Litany of Our Lady (Loreto)

Lord, have mercy.	—Lord, have mercy.
Christ, have mercy.	—Christ, have mercy.
Lord, have mercy.	—Lord, have mercy.

God our Father in heaven,	—Have mercy on us.
God the Son, Redeemer of the world,	—Have mercy on us.
God the Holy Spirit,	—Have mercy on us.
Holy Trinity, one God,	—Have mercy on us.

Holy Mary, —Pray for us.
Holy Mother of God,
Most honored of virgins,

Mother of Christ,
Mother of the Church,
Mother of divine grace,
Mother most pure,
Mother of chaste love,
Mother and virgin,
Sinless Mother,
Dearest of mothers,
Model of motherhood,
Mother of good counsel,
Mother of our Creator,
Mother of our Savior,
Virgin most wise,
Virgin rightly praised,

Virgin rightly renowned,
Virgin most powerful,
Virgin gentle in mercy,
Faithful virgin,
Mirror of justice,
Throne of wisdom,
Cause of our joy,

Shrine of the Spirit,
Glory of Israel,
Vessel of selfless devotion,
Mystical rose,
Tower of David,
Tower of ivory,
House of gold,
Ark of the covenant,
Gate of heaven,
Morning Star,
Health of the sick,
Refuge of sinners,
Comfort of the troubled,
Help of Christians,

Queen of angels,
Queen of patriarchs and prophets,
Queen of apostles and martyrs,
Queen of confessors and virgins,
Queen of all saints,
Queen conceived in grace,

Queen raised up to glory,
Queen of the rosary,
Queen of peace,

Lamb of God, you take away the sins of the world,
　　　　　　　—Have mercy on us.
Lamb of God, you take away the sins of the world,
　　　　　　　—Have mercy on us.
Lamb of God, you take away the sins of the world,
　　　　　　　—Have mercy on us.

Pray for us, holy Mother of God,
　　—That we may become worthy of the promises
　　of Christ.

Let us pray.

Eternal God,
let your people enjoy constant health in mind
　　　　and body.
Through the intercession of the Virgin Mary
free us from the sorrows of this life
and lead us to happiness in the life to come.
Grant this through Christ our Lord.
—Amen.

Note: A Marian litany containing some of these invocations was in use
in the twelfth century. In its present form, it was approved by Pope Sixtus
V (1585-1590).

Litany of the Blessed Virgin Mary

Lord, have mercy.   —Lord, have mercy
Christ, have mercy.   —Christ, have mercy
Lord, have mercy.   —Lord, have mercy

God our Father in heaven, —Have mercy on us.
God the Son, Redeemer of the world,
       —Have mercy on us.
God the Holy Spirit, —Have mercy on us.
Holy Trinity, one God, —Have mercy on us.

Holy Mary,   —Pray for us.
Holy Mother of God,   —Pray for us.
Most honored of virgins, —Pray for us.
Chosen daughter of the Father,
Mother of Christ the King,
Glory of the Holy Spirit,

Virgin daughter of Zion,
Virgin poor and humble,
Virgin gentle and obedient,

Handmaid of the Lord,
Mother of the Lord,
Helper of the Redeemer,

Full of grace,
Fountain of beauty,
Model of virtue,

Finest fruit of the redemption,
Perfect disciple of Christ,
Untarnished image of the Church,

Woman transformed,
Woman clothed with the sun,
Woman crowned with stars,

Gentle lady,
Gracious lady,
Our Lady,

Joy of Israel,
Splendor of the Church,
Pride of the human race,

Advocate of peace,
Minister of holiness,
Champion of God's people,

Queen of love,
Queen of mercy,
Queen of peace,

Queen of angels,
Queen of patriarchs and prophets,
Queen of apostles and martyrs,
Queen of confessors and virgins,

Queen of all saints,
Queen conceived without original sin,
Queen assumed into heaven,

Queen of all the earth,
Queen of heaven,
Queen of the universe,

Lamb of God, you take away
　　the sins of the world,　—Spare us, O Lord.
Lamb of God, you take away
　　the sins of the world,　　—Hear us, O Lord.
Lamb of God, you take away
　　the sins of the world, —Have mercy on us.

Pray for us, O glorious Mother of the Lord.
　—That we may become worthy of the promises
　　of Christ.

Let us pray.
God of mercy,
listen to the prayers of your servants
who have honored your handmaid Mary
      as mother and queen.
Grant that by your grace
we may serve you and our neighbor on earth
and be welcomed into your eternal kingdom.
We ask this through Christ our Lord.
—Amen.

Text: Approved by the Bishops' Committee on the Liturgy, National Conference of Roman Catholic Bishops U.S.A., March 23, 1987. *Book of Mary* (Washington D.C.: United States Catholic Conference, 1987), p. 27.

Litany of St. Joseph

Lord, have mercy.	—Lord, have mercy.
Christ, have mercy.	—Christ have mercy.
Lord, have mercy.	—Lord, have mercy.

God our Father in heaven,	—Have mercy on us.
God the Son, Redeemer of the world,	—Have mercy on us.
God the Holy Spirit,	—Have mercy on us.
Holy Trinity, one God,	—Have mercy on us.

St. Joseph,	—Pray for us.
Noble son of the House of David,	

Light of patriarchs,
Husband of the Mother of God,
Guardian of the Virgin,
Foster-father of the Son of God,
Faithful guardian of Christ,
Head of the holy family,

Joseph, chaste and just,
Joseph, prudent and brave,
Joseph, obedient and loyal,
Pattern of patience,
Lover of poverty,
Model of workers,
Example to parents,
Guardian of virgins,
Pillar of family life,
Comfort of the troubled,
Hope of the sick,
Patron of the dying,
Terror of evil spirits,
Protector of the Church.

Lamb of God, you take away the sins of the world,
— Have mercy on us.
Lamb of God, you take away the sins of the world,
— Have mercy on us.
Lamb of God, you take away the sins of the world,
— Have mercy on us.

God made him master of his household,
—And put him in charge of all that he owned.

Let us pray.

Almighty God,
in your infinite wisdom and love
you chose Joseph to be the husband of Mary,
the mother of your Son.
As we enjoy his protection on earth
may we have the help of his prayers in heaven.
We ask this through Christ our Lord.
—Amen.

Note: Text approved by Pope Pius X (1903-1914).

Byzantine Litany

In peace, let us pray to the Lord.

—Lord, have mercy.

For peace from on high and for the salvation of
our souls,
let us pray to the Lord.

—Lord, have mercy.

For peace throughout the world, the welfare of
God's Church,
and the unity of the human race,
let us pray to the Lord.

—Lord, have mercy.

For this holy place and for all those who gather here
    in faith, reverence and fear of God,
let us pray to the Lord.
                          —Lord, have mercy.
For our holy father, *Name*, for our bishop, *Name*,
    and for our pastor, *Name*,
    and for all the clergy and people,
let us pray to the Lord.
                          —Lord, have mercy.
For this nation, its government,
    and for all who serve and protect us,
let us pray to the Lord.
                          —Lord, have mercy.
For this city and for every human habitation
    and for all those living in them,
let us pray to the Lord.
                          —Lord, have mercy.
For seasonable weather, bountiful harvests,
    and for peaceful times,
let us pray to the Lord.
                          —Lord, have mercy.
For the safety of travelers, the recovery of the sick,
    the liberation of the oppressed,
    and the release of prisoners,
let us pray to the Lord.
                          —Lord, have mercy.

For our deliverance from all affliction,
    anger, danger and need,
let us pray to the Lord.

                              —Lord, have mercy.

Help, save, pity and defend us,
    O God, by your grace.

(spontaneous prayer)

As we remember the great Mother of God, Mary
        most holy,
Saint *Name*, and all the saints,
let us commend ourselves, one another,
and our whole life to Christ our Lord.
—To you, O Lord.

Prayer

By your grace, O God,
we make these common prayers
with one accord,
calling to mind the promise of your Son
that you will grant the requests
of two or three gathered together in your name.
Answer our prayers now, O Lord,
as may be most expedient for us,
granting us in this world knowledge of your truth
and in the world to come life everlasting;
for all glory, honor and worship belong to you,

Father, Son and Holy Spirit,
now and always and for ever and ever.
—Amen.

Text: Translation adapted from the Byzantine Liturgy.

Ask, and you shall receive;
Seek, and you shall find;
Knock, and the door shall be opened for you.

(Matthew 7:7)

7. Eucharistic Devotions

The Lord's Supper on the Lord's Day is the central liturgical action of God's people. In the eucharistic celebration we listen as God speaks to us in the Bible readings and the homily; we pray for our needs, general and particular; and we praise and thank our heavenly Father for all that he has done for us in Christ, for all that he is doing for us this very day, and for all that he promises to do for us in the days to come. We ratify and complete all this by eating and drinking his sacramental body and blood in a holy communion: "the gifts of God for the people of God."

This communal act of worship and dedication is prolonged, so to speak, in the sacrament reserved primarily for the sick and dying *(viaticum)*. Over the centuries the tabernacle has become the focus of many forms of devotion, reminding us continually of Jesus' abiding presence with his Church and extending the grace of the sacrifice to all the hours of the day and night.

The prayers included here may be used before or after Mass, in preparation and thanksgiving for home communion for the sick and dying, and for private visits to the Blessed Sacrament. The Hours of the Blessed Sacrament (pp. 157, 163) are also be suitable for visits.

Hymn to the Blessed Sacrament

Godhead here in hiding, whom I do adore
Masked by these bare shadows, shape and
nothing more,
See, Lord, at thy service low lies here a heart
Lost, all lost in wonder at the God thou art.

Seeing, touching, tasting are in thee deceived;
How says trusty hearing? That shall be believed;
What God's Son has told me, take for truth I do;
Truth himself speaks truly or there's nothing true.

On the cross thy godhead made no sign to men;
Here thy very manhood steals from human ken:
Both are my confession, both are my belief,
And I pray the prayer of the dying thief.

I am not like Thomas, wounds I cannot see,
But can plainly call thee Lord and God as he:

This faith each day deeper be my holding of,
Daily make me harder hope and dearer love.

O thou our reminder of Christ crucified,
Living Bread the life of us for whom he died,
Lend this life to me then: feed and feast my mind,
There be thou the sweetness man was meant to find.

Bring the tender tale true of the Pelican;
Bathe me, Jesu Lord, in what thy bosom ran—
Blood that but one drop of has the world to win
All the world forgiveness of its world of sin.

Jesu whom I look at shrouded here below,
I beseech thee send me what I thirst for so,
Some day to gaze on thee face to face in light
And be blest for ever with thy glory's sight.

Text: Adoro te devote, attributed to St. Thomas Aquinas, O.P. (1225-1274), trans. Gerard Manley Hopkins, S.J.

Sing, My Tongue, the Savior's Glory

Hail our Savior's glorious Body,
Which his Virgin Mother bore;
Hail the Blood which, shed for sinners,
Did a broken world restore;
Hail the sacrament most holy,
Flesh and blood of Christ adore!

To the Virgin, for our healing,
His own Son the Father sends;
From the Father's love proceeding
Sower, seed and Word descends;
Wondrous life of Word incarnate
With his greatest wonder ends!

On that paschal evening see him
With the chosen twelve recline,
To the old law still obedient
In its feast of love divine;
Love divine, the new law giving,
Gives himself as Bread and Wine!

By his word the Word almighty
Makes of bread his flesh indeed;
Wine becomes his very life-blood:
Faith God's living Word must heed!
Faith alone may safely guide us
Where the senses cannot lead!

Come, adore this wondrous presence;
Bow to Christ, the source of grace!
Here is kept the ancient promise
Of God's earthly dwelling-place!
Sight is blind before God's glory,
Faith alone may see his face!

Glory be to God the Father,
Praise to his co-equal Son,
Adoration to the Spirit,
Bond of love, in Godhead one!
Blest be God by all creation
Joyously while ages run!

Text: *Pange lingua gloriosi,* by St. Thomas Aquinas, O.P. (1225-1274), trans.
James Quinn, S.J., *Praise for All Seasons,* p. 59.

Prayer Before Mass

Almighty and ever-living God,
I approach the sacrament of your
          only-begotten Son,
our Lord Jesus Christ.
I come unclean to the fountain of mercy,
blind to the radiance of eternal light,
poor and needy to the Lord of heaven and earth.

Lord, in your great generosity,
heal my sickness, wash away my defilement,
enlighten my blindness, enrich my poverty,
and clothe my nakedness.

May I receive the bread of angels,
the King of kings and Lord of lords,
with humble reverence,

with the purity and faith,
the repentance and love,
and the determined purpose
that will help to bring me to salvation.
May I receive the sacrament
of the Lord's body and blood,
and its reality and power.

Kind God,
may I receive the body
of your only-begotten Son, our Lord Jesus Christ,
born from the womb of the Virgin Mary,
and so be received into his mystical body,
and numbered among his members.
Loving Father,
as on my earthly pilgrimage
I now receive your beloved Son
under the veil of a sacrament,
may I one day see him face to face in glory,
who lives and reigns with you for ever. Amen.

Text: Attributed to St. Thomas Aquinas, O.P. (1225-1274), *The Book of Prayers* (Washington D.C.; ICEL, 1982) p. 4.

Prayer After Mass

Lord, Father all-powerful, and ever-living God,
I thank you,
for even though I am a sinner, your
       unprofitable servant,
not because of my worth, but in the kindness of
       your mercy,
you have fed me
with the precious body and blood of your Son,
       our Lord Jesus Christ.

I pray that this holy communion
may not bring me condemnation and punishment,
but forgiveness and salvation.
May it be a helmet of faith
and a shield of good will.
May it purify me from evil ways
and put an end to my evil passions.
May it bring me charity and patience,
humility and obedience,
and growth in the power to do good.
May it be my strong defense
against all my enemies, visible and invisible,
and the perfect calming of all my evil impulses,
bodily and spiritual.
May it unite me more closely to you,
the one true God,

and lead me safely through death
to everlasting happiness with you.
And I pray that you will lead me, a sinner,
to the banquet where you,
with your Son and Holy Spirit,
are true and perfect light,
total fulfillment, everlasting joy,
gladness without end,
and perfect happiness to your saints.
Grant this through Christ our Lord. Amen.

Text: Attributed to St. Thomas Aquinas, O.P. (1225-1274), *The Book of Prayers* (Washington D.C.; ICEL, 1982), p. 9.

Jesus Our Delight

Jesus to cast one thought upon
makes gladness after he is gone;
but more than honey and honeycomb
is to come near and take him home.

Song never was so sweet in ear,
word never was such news to hear,
thought half so sweet there is not one
as Jesus God the Father's Son.

Jesu, their hope who go astray,
so kind to those who ask the way,

so good to those who look for Thee,
to those who find what must Thou be?

To speak of that no tongue will do
nor letters suit to spell it true;
but they can guess who have tasted of
what Jesus is and what is love.

Jesu, a springing well thou art,
daylight to head and treat to heart,
and matched with thee there's nothing glad
that we have wished for or have had.

Wish us good morning when we wake
and light us, Lord, with thy day-break.
Beat from our brains the thicky night
and fill the world up with delight.

Be our delight, O Jesu, now
as by and by our prize art thou,
and grant our glorying may be
world without end alone in thee.

Text: *Jesu dulcis memoria*, 12th century Latin hymn, trans. Gerard Manley Hopkins.

Antiphon and Prayers

How holy this feast in which Christ is our food;
his passion is recalled;
grace fills our hearts;
and we receive a pledge of the glory to come.

I am the living bread come down from heaven.
—Anyone who eats this bread will live for ever.

Let us pray.

Lord Jesus Christ,
you gave us the Eucharist
as the memorial of your suffering and death.
May our worship of this sacrament of your body
        and blood
help us to experience the salvation you won for us
and the peace of the kingdom,
where you live with the Father and the Holy Spirit,
one God, for ever and ever.
—Amen.

or:

Lord Jesus Christ,
we worship you living among us
in the sacrament of your body and blood.
May we offer to our Father in heaven
a solemn pledge of undivided love.
May we offer to our brothers and sisters

a life poured out in loving service of that kingdom,
where you live with the Father and the Holy Spirit,
one God, for ever and ever.
—Amen.

or:

Almighty God,
we offer you our souls and bodies
to be a living sacrifice
through Jesus Christ our Lord.
Send us into the world in the power of your Spirit,
to live and work for your praise and glory.
—Amen.

To Jesus Living in Mary

Jesu that dost in Mary dwell,
be in thy servants' hearts as well,
in the spirit of thy holiness,
in the fullness of thy force and stress,
in the very ways that thy life goes,
and virtues that thy pattern shows,
in the sharing of thy mysteries;
and every power in us that is
against thy power put under feet
in the Holy Ghost the Paraclete
to the glory of the Father. Amen.

Text: Charles de Condren (1588-1641), trans. Gerard Manley Hopkins, S.J.

O God I Love Thee

O God, I love thee, I love thee—
not out of hope of heaven for me
nor fearing not to love and be
in the everlasting burning.
Thou, thou, my Jesus, after me
didst reach thine arms out dying,
for my sake sufferedst nails and lance,
mocked and marr'd countenance,
sorrows passing number,
sweat and care and cumber,
yea and death, and this for me,
and thou couldst see me sinning:
then I, why should not I love thee,
Jesu, so much in love with me?
Not for heaven's sake; not to be
out of hell by loving thee;
not for any gains I see;
but just the way that thou didst me
I do love and I will love thee:
what must I love thee, Lord, for then?
For being my king and God. Amen.

Text: *O Deus, ego amo te*, by St. Francis Xavier, S.J. (1506-1552), trans. Gerard Manley Hopkins, S.J.

Prayer of Self-Dedication to Jesus Christ

Lord Jesus Christ,
take all my freedom, my memory,
my understanding and my will.
All that I love and cherish
you have given me.
I surrender it all to be guided by your will.
Your grace and your love
are wealth enough for me.
Give me these, Lord Jesus,
and I ask for nothing more

Text: Attributed to Saint Ignatius Loyola, S.J. (1491-1556), *Book of Prayers* (Washington D. C.: ICEL, 1982), p. 10.

Prayer Before a Crucifix

Good Jesus, friend of all,
I kneel before you hanging on the cross
and recall with sorrow and affection
your five precious wounds,
while I ponder the prophetic words
of King David your ancestor:
"They have pierced my hands and my feet
I can count all my bones" (Psalm 22:17).
Good Jesus, crucified for me,
fix this image of yourself in my heart:

fill me with lively sentiments of faith, hope, and love,
make me truly sorry for my sins
and utterly committed to your gospel. Amen.

Text: *En ego, o bone*, 16th century

Prayer to Our Redeemer

Soul of Christ make me holy.
Body of Christ feed me.
Blood of Christ cover me.
Water from Christ's side wash me.
Passion of Christ strengthen me.
O good Jesus hear me.
In your wounds hide me.
From all sin keep me.
From Satan protect me.
At the hour of death call me.
To your side invite me
to praise you with all your saints
for ever and ever.
Amen.

Text: *Anima Christi*, early 14th century.

May the heart of Jesus
in the most Blessed Sacrament of the altar
be praised, adored, and loved
with grateful affection, at every moment,
in all the tabernacles of the world,
even unto the end of time!

Sunday Eucharist

*On the Lord's Day, you should assemble,
break bread, and celebrate the eucharist, but
first having confessed your transgressions,
in order that your sacrifice may be
untainted. No one who has had a quarrel
with a fellow Christian should join your
assembly until they have made up, so that
your sacrifice may not be defiled. For this is
what the Lord meant when he said: "At
every place and time offer me a clean sacrifice, for I am a great king, says the Lord,
and my name is wonderful among the hea-
then" (Malachi 1:11, 14).*

Text: The *Didache* (Teaching), section 14, Syria or Asia Minor; late first
century, trans. Herbert A. Musurillo, S.J., *The Fathers of the Primitive
Church* (New York: New American Library, 1966), p. 61.

8. Reconciliation

"Repent and believe the Good News" (Mark 1:15).

We know we are sinners. Therefore, we seek reconciliation with God and with one another. This entails a radical transformation of our lives—a long process of growth from selfishness to generosity.

The sacrament of penance is an important way to stimulate this growth. By its emphasis on reconciliation and forgiveness, the new Rite of Penance has already proved its worth.

Apart from occasions when we receive this sacrament, we need times when we can look carefully at our lives privately. We discern the Lord's presence there and illuminate the dark side where we have failed to live his law of love.

We can use the following section for help in making this prayerful exploration. Or we may use it to prepare for a devout reception of the sacrament of penance.

Prayer to the Holy Spirit

Come, O Holy Spirit, come.
Come as the wind and cleanse;
come as the fire and burn;
convert and consecrate our lives
to our great good and your great glory;
through Jesus Christ our Lord.
Amen.

Scripture Readings
Matthew 9:9-13

As he passed on from there Jesus saw a man named Matthew at his seat in the custom-house, and said to him, "Follow me"; and Matthew rose and followed him. When Jesus was at table in the house, many bad characters— tax-gatherers and others—were seated with him and his disciples. The Pharisees noticed this, and said to his disciples, "Why is it that your master eats with tax-gatherers and sinners?" Jesus heard it and said, "It is not the healthy that need a doctor, but the sick. Go and learn what that text means, 'I require mercy, not sacrifice.' I did not come to invite virtuous people, but sinners" (New English Bible).

Luke 15:1-10

Another time, the tax-gatherers and other bad characters were all crowding in to listen to him; and the Pharisees and the doctors of the law began grumbling among themselves: "This fellow," they said, "welcomes sinners and eats with them." He answered them with this parable: "If one of you has a hundred sheep and loses one of them, does he not leave the ninety-nine in the open pasture and go after the missing one until he has found it? How delighted he is then! He lifts it on to his shoulders, and home he goes to call his friends and neighbors together. 'Rejoice with me!' he cries. 'I have found my lost sheep.' In the same way, I tell you, there will be greater joy in heaven over one sinner who repents than over ninety-nine righteous people who do not need to repent.

"Or again, if a woman has ten silver pieces and loses one of them, does she not light the lamp, sweep out the house, and look in every corner till she has found it? And when she has, she calls her friends and neighbors together, and says, 'Rejoice with me! I have found the piece that I lost.' In the same way, I tell you, there is joy among the angels of God over one sinner who repents" (NEB).

John 20:19-23

Late that Sunday evening, when the disciples were together behind locked doors, for fear of the Jews, Jesus came and stood among them. "Peace be with you!" he said, and then showed them his hands and his side. So when the disciples saw the Lord, they were filled with joy. Jesus repeated, "Peace be with you!" and said, "As the Father sent me, so I send you." Then he breathed on them, saying, "Receive the Holy Spirit! If you forgive anyone's sins, they stand forgiven; if you pronounce them unforgiven, unforgiven they remain" (NEB).

Reflect on some of these passages for a short time, recalling the great love and forgiveness which the Father has graciously extended to us during our lives. He continues to offer us this forgiveness and asks us to be reconciled with him and with our neighbor. There are many other passages in scripture which can also be used, among them the following:

Luke 5:17-26	Christ forgives and cures the paralytic
Luke 7: 36-50	The Lord and a penitent woman
Luke 15:11-32	The wandering and wasteful son who returned home
Luke 19: 1-10	Jesus and Zacchaeus, the tax collector
John 8:1-11	A woman caught in adultery

Guidelines From Scripture

The Old Law: The Ten Commandments
(Exodus 20:2-17 and Deuteronomy 20:1-17)

1. I, the Lord, am your God. You shall not have other gods besides me.

2. You shall not take the name of the Lord, your God, in vain.

3. Remember to keep holy the Sabbath day.

4. Honor your father and your mother.

5. You shall not kill.

6. You shall not commit adultery.

7. You shall not steal.

8. You shall not bear false witness against your neighbor.

9. You shall not covet your neighbor's wife.

10. You shall not covet anything that belongs to your neighbor.

The New Law: The Great Commandment (Mark 12:28-31)

Then one of the lawyers, who had been listening to these discussions and had noted how well he answered, came forward and asked him, "Which commandment is first of all?" Jesus answered, "The first is, 'Hear, O Israel: the Lord our God is the only Lord; love the Lord your God with all your heart, with all your soul, with all your mind, and with all your strength' The second is this: 'Love your neighbor as yourself.' There is no other commandment greater than these" (NEB).

The New Commandment (John 13:34-35)

"I give you a new commandment: love one another; as I have loved you, so you are to love one another. If there is this love among you, then all will know that you are my disciples" (NEB).

The Beatitudes (Matthew 5:3-10)

1. How blest are those who know their need of God; the kingdom of heaven is theirs.

2. How blest are the sorrowful; they shall find consolation.

3. How blest are those of a gentle spirit; they shall have the earth for their possession.

4. How blest are those who hunger and thirst to see right prevail; they shall be satisfied.

5. How blest are those who show mercy; mercy shall be shown to them.

6. How blest are those whose hearts are pure; they shall see God.

7. How blest are the peacemakers; God shall call them his children.

8. How blest are those who have suffered persecution for the cause of right; the kingdom of heaven is theirs (NEB).

Examination of Conscience

To sin is to break a bond, to destroy a relationship, to withdraw myself from God, my Father, and from his love. . . . A sinful act is less important for the disorder it creates than for what it says about me as a person: Who am I? Whom do I love? What is my attitude toward God?

Walter J. Burghardt, S.J.

I. The Lord says: "Love the Lord your God with your whole heart."

Do I keep God in mind and put him first in my life?
Or am I too caught up in material concerns?
Do I worship God regularly and carefully?
Do I respect his name, or have I dishonored it by using it in anger and carelessness?

Do I try to grow in my understanding of the faith?
Do I pray even when I don't feel like it?
Do I trust God and take seriously enough his
personal love and concern for me?
Do I genuinely repent of my sins and accept God's
free and gracious forgiveness?

II. The Lord says: "Love one another as I have
loved you."

Do I love my family and try to create a happy
home life?
Or am I sometimes thoughtless and even cruel
toward them?
Do I try to maintain and foster friendships and give
genuine respect and support to other people?
Am I fair and honest in my relationships?
Or do I sometimes lie or take unfair advantage of
others by cheating them or stealing from them?
Do I respect the rights and sensitivities of others?
Or do I tend to judge people unfairly or ignore them
because they are different?
Do I honestly try to forgive people who dislike me?
Or have I tried to hurt them by what I've said
or done?
Am I trying to improve the quality of life
around me?

Or do I foul up the environment and waste the good
  things I have?
Do I really care about my country and the good of
  the human community of which I am a part?
Or do I care only about myself and the people
  I know?
Am I concerned for the poor, the hungry, and the
  destitute and for the millions who thirst for
  justice and peace?
Can I contribute more of my time, talents, and
  money to the poor of the world?

III. Jesus says: "Be perfect as your heavenly Father
  is perfect."

Am I working at becoming a better person and a
  better Christian?
Am I making the most of my talents, my education
  and my opportunities?
Or do I fail to use them sometimes?
Do I take care of my body, and make sure I get
  enough sleep and exercise?
Do I eat and drink in moderation?
Am I grateful for my sexuality and anxious to grow
  in sexual maturity and responsibility?
Or do I misuse my sexual powers in selfish or
  exploitative ways?

Am I able to admit my own need for help and to ask
for it?

Do I accept myself, despite my limitations and
weakness?

What is the fundamental orientation of my life?

Prayers of Sorrow and Thanksgiving

Reflection on the following prayers, or others in this
book (cf. especially in the Prayers for All Seasons section,
pp. 33-87) can make us more aware of our need for sorrow . . . and more grateful to God for the forgiveness
which he offers us unceasingly.

Listen to My Prayer

Lord Jesus,
you opened the eyes of the blind,
healed the sick,
forgave the sinful woman,
and after Peter's denial confirmed him in your love.
Listen to my prayer:
forgive all my sins,
renew your love in my heart,
help me to live in perfect unity with my
        fellow Christians
that I may proclaim your saving power to
        all the world.

Text: Rite of Penance

Fill Our Hearts With Faith

Lord God,
creator and ruler of your kingdom of light,
in your great love for this world
you gave up your only Son
for our salvation.
His cross has redeemed us,
his death has given us life,
his resurrection has raised us to glory.
Through him we ask you
to be always present among your family.
Teach us to be reverent in the presence of
        your glory;
fill our hearts with faith,
our days with good works,
our lives with your love;
may your truth be on our lips
and your wisdom in all our actions,
that we may receive the reward of everlasting life.
We ask this through Christ our Lord. Amen.

Psalm 103:1-4, 8-18   Thanks Be to God!

Praise the Lord, my soul!
All my being, praise his holy name!
Praise the Lord, my soul,
and do not forget how kind he is.
He forgives all my sins
and heals all my diseases.
He keeps me from the grave
and blesses me with love and mercy.
He fills my life with good things,
so that I stay young and strong like an eagle.

The Lord is merciful and loving,
slow to become angry and full of constant love.
He does not keep on rebuking;
he is not angry for ever.
He does not punish us as we deserve
or repay us according to our sins and wrongs.

As high as the sky is above the earth,
so great is his love for those who honor him.
As far as the east is from the west,
so far does he remove our sins from us.
As a father is kind to his children,
so the Lord is kind to those who honor him.
He knows what we are made of;
he remembers that we are dust.

As for us, our life is like grass.
We grow and flourish like a wild flower;
then the wind blows on it—
no one sees it again.
But for those who honor the Lord,
his love lasts for ever,
and his goodness endures for all generations
of those who are true to his covenant
and who faithfully obey his commands.

Let your prayer be completely simple, for both the Publican and the Prodigal Son were reconciled to God by a single phrase.

John Climacus (ca. 559-649)

9. Meditative Prayer

After a long day of preaching and healing, the gospels tell us that Jesus would go off by himself and pray to his Father. What was this prayer like? It must have been an intimate sharing with his Father, a sharing which included praise, thanksgiving, and an urgent plea for guidance to understand and carry out his mission.

We also have a similar need to share intimately with the Father as well as with the risen Lord himself. Harried and scattered as we are by the frenetic pace of our lives, we need to be refreshed by prayerful reflection in solitude. This is what we mean by the term "meditative prayer."

Too often we think that meditative prayer is a luxury reserved for monks and mystics. Not so. More and more Christians are realizing that they not only are called on to spend time daily in meditative prayer, but also are finding that this prayer helps them grow steadily in their union with God.

Where to begin? Reflection on a passage in the Bible is an obvious possibility. For example, consider the following passage from Luke 12:

> Then Jesus said to his disciples, "This is why I am telling you not to worry about your life and what you are to eat, nor about your body and how you are to clothe it. For life means more than food and the body more than clothing. Think of the ravens. They do not sow or reap; they have no storehouses and no barns; yet God feeds them. And how much more are you worth than the birds!" (Luke 12, 22-25, JB).

We know that Jesus intended those words not only for his listeners on that day long ago, but for the millions who would hear and read them down through the centuries. In a deeply personal way he directs those words to you and me.

With this in mind, we read over the passage two or three times and ask the Lord to enlighten us. What does he want us to hear today as we once more dwell on these familiar words? As we try to answer that question, we are drawn into a very personal application of that passage to our lives. Our reflection would not be spoken aloud, much less written down; but if it were jotted down later it might come out looking like this:

Lord, once more I read these words and I realize that I am caught up in all sorts of worries. Worries about my family, my job, my health. Are you telling me to relax and trust more in you? I think you are. Lord, I praise and thank you for pledging yourself to take care of me and the people I love. How great it is to hear that you regard me as a valuable person, and love me! I rejoice, too, at the beautiful picture you give me of the ravens. Outside my window now I see countless beauties of nature which come from the Father. I hear birds outside who, like the ravens, are not sowing or reaping but are simply *living!* And Lord, you do feed them, don't you?

Nevertheless, Lord, you'll forgive me if I simply call your attention to the needs I have, trusting that you will take care of them as you take care of the birds. I'm thinking of that operation which my mother faces next week and our bank account which has never been lower.

Lord, I praise and thank you and promise to trust in you throughout this busy day. Help me to make this passage live today in my heart and in my life.

Depending on our mood and the inspiration of the Spirit, the reflection might take this course; or it might go in a completely different direction. In any event, the passage could well provide food for meditative prayer for a few minutes or a much longer time. The important point is that we would be making that Bible passage part of ourselves and seeking to enflesh it in our lives. Thus does the Lord speak to us!

Sometimes a simple phrase from scripture can trigger a deep experience of meditative prayer. "Young man, I tell you to get up," Jesus says to the dead young man of Nain (Luke 7:15). How easy for a young man (or young woman) today to identify with that command! The meditation might go like this:

> Lord, I am a lot like that young man. True, I'm not dead physically. Nor am I dead spiritually either, as far as I know. I'm not the world's greatest sinner or anything like that! But I am so selfish and self-centered that it amazes me at times. Like the young man, I too need to be *raised up*. Help me to be more aware of my parents and brothers and sisters; help me to be more sensitive to the moods of my friends.

Nudged by the Lord, the young person might then become much more specific about virtues such as courage and patience which he or she needs in great supply at that particular moment. Or the meditation might take a different turn suggested by the Lord. In any event it could be a rich experience of prayer touched off by a single phrase.

To take another example, who can fail to see himself or herself in Cleopas and his companion? On their way to Emmaus, they journeyed for some time with a mysterious stranger and never guessed he was the risen Lord until they broke bread with him. Afterward, they puzzled over their blindness: "Did our hearts not burn within us as he talked to us on the road and explained the scriptures to us?" (Luke 24:32).

Struck by that remark, we might find ourselves meditating on how we are equally blind. We might reflect to ourselves,

> How often, Lord, have I failed to see you in the most obvious places, for example in the persons of my own family? I need special help to see you in those close to me, especially when they get on my nerves like they did yesterday. For that matter I need to see you also in those who are not close to me at all—that poor old woman I passed by so quickly today on my way home from town.

Meditating on this incident and the outcry of the two men might open us to the call of the Lord. He is always challenging us to be more alert to his presence in precisely those persons in whom we have the greatest trouble locating him.

In short, by spending time daily in reflection on the gospels, the psalms, the letters of Paul, etc. we gradually come more and more in contact with God and apply his word more and more to our lives. Scripture is a storehouse of riches for meditative prayer.

But reflection on a passage in the Bible is not the only entry to meditative prayer. One of the oldest and simplest ways is the Jesus Prayer, which can be traced back to the early centuries of the Church. By repeatedly invoking the name of Jesus, Christians find they can penetrate deeply into the presence of God who saves and sanctifies. The name of Jesus is sometimes repeated by itself or inserted in a phrase like—Lord Jesus Christ, Son of the living God, have mercy on me, a sinner.

The best way to say the Jesus prayer is to sit in as much physical and inner stillness as we can manage and to repeat the invocation over and over, slowly and insistently. We fix our attention directly on the words of the prayer itself, without trying to form images or ideas. In a way we thus "clear away" the concerns which occupy our every waking moment, and allow the Lord to speak to us. As we pronounce the name of Jesus with deep reverence and faith, we bring his presence and power into our lives.

Many Christians spend a definite period of time each day on the Jesus Prayer and find that it becomes the very substance of their prayer life. For them, it is much more than a mechanical repetition of a word or phrase; it is a practice of meditative prayer which leads to a deep union with Jesus and with his Father.

A similar entry to meditative prayer is described in *The Cloud of Unknowing*, a book by an anonymous English

Catholic writer of the fourteenth century. Called "centering prayer" by some, this simple method resembles the Jesus Prayer but comes out of a different time and tradition. We find a quiet place and sit comfortably with our eyes closed. We center all our attention and desire on God dwelling within us, turning ourselves over to him, and remaining quietly in his presence. Then we respond to God's presence with a single word like "God" or "love" and let this word repeat itself within us, focusing on the word and not trying to summon up ideas or images.

Whenever we become aware of distractions, we calmly turn back to the prayer word and continue to abide in God's presence. At the end of twenty minutes or so, we conclude with an Our Father which is said slowly and reflectively.

Like those who use the Jesus Prayer, Christians who are drawn to the centering prayer frequently find that their union with God has deepened immensely. They discover a dimension to prayer which has eluded them until then.

Scripture reflection, the Jesus Prayer or the centering prayer of *The Cloud of Unknowing* are practical approaches to meditative prayer. Others meditate by saying very slowly classic prayers such as the Lord's Prayer or the Creed, or by means of such devotions as the Rosary or the Way of the Cross. Still others will find material for reflection in other prayers in this book.

For example, a wealth of material may be found in The Year of Our Lord (pp. 195-269) and The Week With Christ (pp. 89-193). A particular psalm, poem, or prayer in those sections may trigger a period of meditative prayer for us. Other forms of prayer may also do the same for us: one of the familiar Everyday Prayers (pp. 15-31), for instance, or one of the Prayers for All Seasons (pp. 33-87). Those attempting the Centering Prayer will find many useful words or phrases in the litanies (pp. 285-313).

No matter what the approach we favor, or where we look for material for reflection, we are urged to spend a certain period of time daily at meditative prayer. Generally, it is far better to spend five minutes a day *each* day than a half-hour one day and nothing the next. Most of us find it convenient to set aside a particular time daily, perhaps early in the morning or just before bed at night. It is also a good idea to set aside a certain place, a "prayer nook" which is accessible even when privacy is at a premium. Finally, we must remind ourselves that sometimes we will feel the time we spend is utterly wasted—"Nothing is happening!" At those times we must simply wait on the Lord in patience and trust. After all, the work of prayer is not really our work but his, and if he should wish to give us times of dryness that's his business and not ours.

Such times of dryness will not last long. The Lord is a gracious giver and will not be surpassed in generosity.

As we set aside time and space for meditative prayer we will find him drawing closer to us and lighting up our lives in ways we never imagined.

> *Let us meditate on the gospels. Amidst the confusion of so many human words, the gospel is the only voice that enlightens and attracts, that consoles and quenches thirst.*

Pope John XXIII (1958-1963)

10. The Way of the Cross

Pilgrims to Jerusalem and its holy places brought back to Europe the pious custom of visiting in prayer the spots especially associated with the passion, death, and burial of Jesus. Churches, monasteries, and shrines began to erect Stations of the Cross to facilitate preaching and meditation on the Man of Sorrows and his slow way from the court of Pilate to Golgotha and the Tomb.

In the eighteenth century St. Leonard Casanova (1676-1751), a famed Franciscan preacher who drew enormous crowds to his sermons, promoted this devotion all over Italy, setting up some 600 sets of stations. His devotional success encouraged the spread of the Way of the Cross throughout the Catholic world until today no Catholic parish is without a set of stations.

The Way of the Cross which follows is primarily for private meditation. We can use it before a crucifix in the privacy of our homes or in a church or chapel where there are stations which depict these episodes. This devotion will not only help us enter into the sufferings of Jesus but also into the whole world of suffering humanity in whom the passion is still being realized.

Stations of the Cross

Jesus said to the people of his time, "If you want to be my disciples, take up your cross and come follow me." Today in young people of the world, Jesus lives his Passion, in the suffering, in the hungry, the handicapped young people—in that child who eats a piece of bread crumb by crumb, because when that piece of bread is finished, there will be no more and hunger will come again.

That is a Station of the Cross.

Are you there with that child?

And those thousands who die not only for a piece of bread, but for a little bit of love, of recognition. That is a Station of the Cross. Are you there?

And young people, when they fall, as Jesus fell again and again for us, are we there as Simon of Cyrene to pick them up, to pick up the Cross?

The people in the parks, the alcoholics, the homeless, they are looking for you. Do not be those who look but do not see.

Look and see.

Text: Mother Teresa of Calcutta in Eileen Egan, *Such a Vision of the Street* (New York: Doubleday and Co., 1985), pp. 282-283.

First Station: Pontius Pilate Condemns Jesus to Crucifixion

We adore you, O Christ, and we bless you,
—For by your holy cross you have redeemed
the world.

Pilate wanted to please the crowd, so he set Barabbas free for them. Then he had Jesus whipped and handed him over to be crucified. The soldiers took Jesus inside the courtyard of the governor's palace and called together the rest of the company. They put a purple robe on Jesus, made a crown of thorny branches, and put it on his head. Then they began to salute him: "Long live the King of the Jews." They beat him over the head with a stick, spat on him, fell on their knees, and bowed down to him (Mark 15:15-19).

silent meditation

Lord Jesus crucified, have mercy on us sinners.
—Mary, Mother of Sorrows, pray for us.

Second Station: Jesus Carries His Cross

We adore you, O Christ, and we bless you,
—For by your holy cross you have redeemed
the world.

When the soldiers had finished making fun of him, they took off the purple robe and put his own clothes back on him. Then they led him out to crucify him (Mark 15:20).

silent meditation

Lord Jesus crucified, have mercy on us sinners.
—Mary, Mother of Sorrows, pray for us.

Third Station: Jesus Falls the First Time

We adore you, O Christ, and we bless you,
—For by your holy cross you have redeemed
   the world.

Jesus threw himself on the ground and prayed that, if possible, he might not have to go through that time of suffering. "Father," he prayed, "My Father! All things are possible for you. Take this cup of suffering away from me. Yet not what I want, but what you want" (Mark 14:35-36).

silent meditation

Lord Jesus crucified, have mercy on us sinners.
—Mary, Mother of Sorrows, pray for us.

Fourth Station: Jesus Meets His Mother Mary

We adore you, O Christ, and we bless you,
—For by your holy cross you have redeemed the world.

Simeon said to Mary, his mother, "This child is chosen by God for the destruction and the salvation of many in Israel. He will be a sign from God which many people will speak against and so reveal their secret thoughts. And sorrow, like a sharp sword, will break your own heart" (Luke 2:34-35).

silent meditation

Lord Jesus crucified, have mercy on us sinners.
—Mary, Mother of Sorrows, pray for us.

Fifth Station: Simon of Cyrene

We adore you, O Christ, and we bless you,
—For by your holy cross you have redeemed the world.

The soldiers led Jesus away, and as they were going they met a man from Cyrene named Simon who was coming into the city from the country. They seized him, put the cross on him, and made him carry it behind Jesus (Luke 23:26).

silent meditation

Lord Jesus crucified, have mercy on us sinners.
—Mary, Mother of Sorrows, pray for us.

Sixth Station: The Face of Jesus
We adore you, O Christ, and we bless you,
—For by your holy cross you have redeemed the world.

He had no dignity or beauty to make us take notice of him. There was nothing attractive about him, nothing that would draw us to him. We despised and rejected him; he endured suffering and pain. No one would even look at him. We ignored him as if he were nothing (Isaiah 53:2-3).

silent meditation

Lord Jesus crucified, have mercy on us sinners.
—Mary, Mother of Sorrows, pray for us.

Seventh Station: Jesus Falls a Second Time
We adore you, O Christ, and we bless you,
—For by your holy cross you have redeemed the world.

He endured the suffering that should have been ours, the pain that we should have borne. . . . But because of our sins he was wounded, beaten because of the evil we did. We are healed by the punishment he suffered, made whole by the blows he received. All of us were like sheep that were lost, each of us going his own way. But the Lord made the punishment fall on him, the punishment all of us deserved (Isaiah 53:4-6).

silent meditation

Lord Jesus crucified, have mercy on us sinners.
—Mary, Mother of Sorrows, pray for us.

Eighth Station: Jesus Speaks to the Women of Jerusalem

We adore you, O Christ, and we bless you,
—For by your holy cross you have redeemed the world.

A large crowd of people followed Jesus; among them were some women who were weeping and wailing for him. Jesus turned to them and said. "Women of Jerusalem! Don't cry for me, but for yourselves and your children. For the days are coming when people will say, 'How lucky are the women who never had children, who never bore babies, who never nursed them!' That will be

LORD HEAR OUR PRAYER

the time when people will say to the mountains, 'Fall on us!' and to the hills, 'Hide us!' For if such things as these are done when the wood is green, what will happen when it is dry?" (Luke 23:27-31).

silent meditation

Lord Jesus crucified, have mercy on us sinners.
—Mary, Mother of Sorrows, pray for us.

Ninth Station: Jesus Falls for the Third Time

We adore you, O Christ, and we bless you,
—For by your holy cross you have redeemed the world.

"The hour has now come for the Son of Man to receive great glory. I am telling you the truth: a grain of wheat remains no more than a single grain unless it is dropped into the ground and dies. If it does die, then it produces many grains. Those who love their own life will lose it; those who hate their own life in this world will keep it for life eternal. Whoever wants to serve me must follow me, so that my servant will be with me where I am" (John 12:23-26).

silent meditation

Lord Jesus crucified, have mercy on us sinners.
—Mary, Mother of Sorrows, pray for us.

Tenth Station: Jesus Is Stripped of His Clothes

We adore you, O Christ, and we bless you,

—For by your holy cross you have redeemed the world.

The soldiers took Jesus to a place called Golgotha, which means, "The Place of the Skull." There they tried to give him wine mixed with a drug called myrrh, but Jesus would not drink it. Then they crucified him and divided his clothes among themselves, throwing dice to see who would get which piece of clothing (Mark 15:22-24).

silent meditation

Lord Jesus crucified, have mercy on us sinners.

—Mary, Mother of Sorrows, pray for us.

Eleventh Station: Jesus Is Nailed to the Cross

We adore you, O Christ, and we bless you,

—For by your holy cross you have redeemed the world.

Two other men, both of them criminals, were also led out to be put to death with Jesus. When they came to the place called "The Skull," they crucified Jesus there, and the two criminals, one on his right and the other on his left. Jesus said, "Forgive them, Father! They don't know what they are doing. . . ."

The people stood there watching while the Jewish leaders made fun of him: "He saved others; let him save himself if he is the Messiah whom God has chosen!" The soldiers also made fun of him: they came up to him and offered him cheap wine, and said, "Save yourself if you are the king of the Jews!"

Above him were written these words: "This is Jesus of Nazareth, the King of the Jews." One of the criminals hanging there hurled insults at him: "Aren't you the Messiah? Save yourself and us!" The other one, however, rebuked him, saying, "Don't you fear God? You received the same sentence he did. Ours, however, is only right, because we are getting what we deserve for what we did; but he has done no wrong." And he said to Jesus, "Remember me, Jesus, when you come as King!" Jesus said to him, "I promise you that today you will be in Paradise with me" (Luke 23:32-43).

silent meditation

Lord Jesus crucified, have mercy on us sinners.
—Mary, Mother of Sorrows, pray for us.

Twelfth Station: Jesus Dies on the Cross

We adore you, O Christ, and we bless you,
—For by your holy cross you have redeemed the world.

Standing close to Jesus' cross were his mother, his mother's sister Mary the wife of Clopas, and Mary Magdalene. Jesus saw his mother and the disciple he loved standing there; so he said to his mother, "He is your son." Then he said to his disciple, "She is your mother." From that time the disciple took her to live in his home (John 19:25-27).

It was about twelve o'clock when the sun stopped shining and darkness covered the whole country until three o'clock; and the curtain hanging in the Temple was torn in two. Jesus cried out in a loud voice, "Father! In your hands I place my spirit!" He said this and died (Luke 23:44-45).

When the soldiers came to Jesus, they saw that he was already dead, so they did not break his legs. One of the soldiers, however, plunged his spear into Jesus' side, and at once blood and water poured out (John 19:33-34).

silent meditation

Lord Jesus crucified, have mercy on us sinners.
—Mary, Mother of Sorrows, pray for us.

Thirteenth Station: Jesus Is Taken Down From the Cross

We adore you, O Christ, and we bless you,

—For by your holy cross you have redeemed the world.

When the army officer and the soldiers with him who were watching Jesus saw the earthquake and everything else that happened, they were terrified and said, "He really was the Son of God!" (Matthew 27:54). When the people who had gathered there to watch the spectacle saw what had happened, they all went back home, beating their breasts in sorrow. All those who knew Jesus personally, including the women who had followed him from Galilee, stood at a distance to watch (Luke 23:48-49).

silent meditation

Lord Jesus crucified, have mercy on us sinners.

—Mary, Mother of Sorrows, pray for us.

Fourteenth Station: Jesus Is Laid in the Tomb

We adore you, O Christ, and we bless you,

—For by your holy cross you have redeemed the world.

There was a man named Joseph from Arimathea, a town in Judea. He was a good and honorable man, who was waiting for the coming of the Kingdom of God. Although he was a member of the Council, he had not agreed with their decision and action. He went into the presence of Pilate and asked for the body of Jesus. Then he took the body down, wrapped it in a linen sheet, and placed it in a tomb which had been dug out of solid rock and which had never been used. It was Friday, and the Sabbath was about to begin.

The women who had followed Jesus from Galilee went with Joseph and saw the tomb and how Jesus' body was placed in it. Then they went back home and prepared the spices and perfumes for the body. On the Sabbath they rested, as the Law commanded (Luke 23:50-56).

silent meditation

Lord Jesus crucified, have mercy on us sinners.
—Mary, Mother of Sorrows, pray for us.

Closing Prayer

We adore your cross, O Lord,
and we praise and glorify your holy resurrection,
for by the wood of the cross
joy came into the whole world.

The Cross and Daily Life

Lord, help us to see in your crucifixion and resurrection an example of how to endure and seemingly to die in the agony and conflict of daily life, so that we may live more fully and creatively. You accepted patiently and humbly the rebuffs of human life, as well as the tortures of your crucifixion and passion. Help us to accept the pains and conflicts that come to us each day as opportunities to grow as people and become more like you. Enable us to go through them patiently and bravely, trusting that you will support us. Make us realize that it is only by frequent deaths of ourselves and our self-centered desires that we can come to live more fully; for it is only by dying with you that we can rise with you.

Text: Mother Teresa of Calcutta, *A Gift for God: Mother Teresa of Calcutta* (New York: Harper and Row Pub., 1975), pp. 73-74.

In every human being there is an abyss that only God can fill.

Blaise Pascal (1623–1662)

11. The Rosary of the Blessed Virgin Mary

The rosary combines vocal prayer and meditation in a simple way suitable to all types of Christians. Its fifteen mysteries are arranged in sets of five, following the sequence of the life of Jesus and that of his Blessed Mother. Each decade of the rosary is composed of one Our Father, ten Hail Marys, and one Glory. Each set of five mysteries is called a chaplet and is preceded by the recitation of the Apostles' Creed, the Lord's Prayer, and three Hail Marys for an increase of faith, hope, and charity. Each chaplet may be concluded with one of the Marian anthems appropriate to the mysteries that were just prayed.

Many people find that adding a line of scripture before each decade and an appropriate phrase to the first half of the Hail Mary each time helps them concentrate their attention on the mystery to be contemplated. The constant repetition of the same vocal prayers, the use of the beads themselves, and the pattern of salutation and response set up a rhythm favorable to peaceful, recollected prayer.

In origin the rosary was a form of private and personal devotion and it's probably still best used in the peace and quiet of solo recitation. Sitting is normally the posture most favorable to the recollection which the rosary fosters.

The Joyful Mysteries
1. The Angel Gabriel's Message to Mary
The Lord himself will give you a sign: a young woman who is pregnant will have a son and name him Immanuel (Isaiah 7:14).

Hail, Mary, full of grace, the Lord is with you.
Blessed are you among women,
and blessed is the fruit of your womb, Jesus,

who was conceived at the message of an angel.

Holy Mary, Mother of God, pray for us sinners,
now and at the hour of our death. Amen.

2. Mary's Visit to Her Cousin Elizabeth

The Lord said to me: "I chose you before I gave you life, and before you were born I selected you to be a prophet to the nations" (Jeremiah 1:5).

Hail, Mary, . . . the fruit of your womb, Jesus,

who consecrated the Baptist in the womb of his mother.

Holy Mary. . . .

3. Jesus' Birth in Bethlehem of Judah

I am here with good news for you, which will bring great joy to all the people. This very day in David's town your Savior was born—Christ the Lord (Luke 2:11-12).

Hail, Mary, . . . the fruit of your womb, Jesus,

who was born for us in the stable of Bethlehem.

4. Jesus Is Presented in the Temple

With my own eyes I have seen your salvation which you have prepared in the presence of all peoples: a light to reveal your will to the Gentiles and bring glory to your people Israel (Luke 2:30-32).

Hail, Mary, . . . the fruit of your womb, Jesus,

the light of the nations and the glory of your people Israel.

5. The Boy Jesus in the Temple

Jesus said to his parents: "Why did you have to look for me? Didn't you know that I had to be in my Father's house?" . . . His mother treasured all these things in her heart (Luke 2:49, 51).

Hail, Mary, . . . the fruit of your womb, Jesus,

the power and the wisdom of God.

After the Joyful Mysteries:
Salve Regina

Mary, our Queen, Mother of mercy,
you are our life, our joy, our hope.
In our exile from Eden
we turn to you as our advocate.
Look on us with eyes of pity,
gentle and loving Mother.
Lead us home at last
into the presence of Jesus.
Blessed is the fruit of your womb,
Mary ever Virgin.

Pray for us, O holy Mother of God,
—that we may become worthy of the promises of Christ.

Let us pray.

Father,
in your plan for our salvation
your Word became flesh,
announced by an angel and born of the Virgin Mary.
May we who believe that she is the mother of God
receive the help of her prayers.
We ask this through Christ our Lord.
—Amen.

The Sorrowful Mysteries
1. The Agony of Jesus in the Garden of Gethsemane

Jesus threw himself on the ground and prayed that, if possible, he might not have to go through that time of suffering. "Abba, dear Father, all things are possible for you. Take this cup of suffering from me. Yet not what I want, but what you want" (Mark 14:35-36).

Hail, Mary, . . . the fruit of your womb Jesus,

who was offered up because he willed it.

LORD HEAR OUR PRAYER

2. The Scourging of Jesus at the Pillar

Pilate wanted to please the crowd, so he set Barabbas free for them. Then he had Jesus whipped and handed him over to be crucified (Mark 15:15).

Hail, Mary, . . . the fruit of your womb, Jesus,

who was bruised for our offenses.

3. The Crowning of Jesus With Thorns

The soldiers made a crown out of thorny branches and put it on his head; then they put a purple robe on him and came to him and said, "Long live the King of the Jews!" And they went up and slapped him (John 19:2-3).

Hail, Mary, . . . the fruit of your womb, Jesus,

a man of sorrows and acquainted with grief.

4. Jesus Walks the Way of the Cross

Pilate handed Jesus over to them to be crucified. So they took charge of Jesus. He went out, carrying his cross, and came to "The Place of the Skull," as it is called. Two other men, both of them criminals, were also led out to be put to death with Jesus (John 19:16-17; Luke 23:32).

Hail, Mary, . . . the fruit of your womb, Jesus,

who was crushed for our sins.

5. Jesus Is Crucified and Dies on the Cross

It was about 12 o'clock when the sun stopped shining, and darkness covered the whole country until three o'clock; and the curtain hanging in the Temple was torn in two. Jesus cried out in a loud voice, "Father, in your hands I place my spirit!" He said this and died (Luke 23:44-46).

Hail, Mary, . . . the fruit of your womb, Jesus,

by whose wounds we are healed.

After the Sorrowful Mysteries:
Sub Tuum Praesidium

We turn to you for protection,
holy Mother of God.
From your place in heaven
help us in all our needs.
Blessed Virgin in glory,
save us from every danger.

Mother of Sorrows, pray for us,
—that we may become worthy of the promises of Christ.

Let us pray.

Father,
as your Son was raised on the cross,
his mother Mary stood by him, sharing his sufferings.
May your Church be united with Christ
in his suffering and death
and so come to share in his rising to new life,
where he lives and reigns with you and the Holy
    Spirit,
one God, for ever and ever.
—Amen.

The Glorious Mysteries

1. Christ Rises From the Grave

"This is what was written: the Messiah must suffer and must rise from death three days later, and in his name the message about repentance and the forgiveness of sins must be preached to all nations" (Luke 24:46-47).

Hail, Mary, . . . the fruit of your womb, Jesus,

who died for our sins and rose for our justification.

2. Christ Ascends Into Heaven

After the Lord Jesus had talked with them, he was taken up to heaven and sat at the right hand of God. The disciples went and preached everywhere and the Lord worked with them and proved that their preaching was true (Mark 16:19-20).

Hail, Mary, . . . the fruit of your womb, Jesus,

who now sits at the right hand of the Father.

3. The Gift of the Holy Spirit

When the Holy Spirit comes upon you, you will be filled with power and you will be witnesses for me . . . to the ends of the earth (Acts 1:8).

Hail, Mary, . . . the fruit of your womb, Jesus,

who sends us the Holy Spirit as he promised.

4. The Falling Asleep and Assumption of Our Lady

What is mortal must be changed into what is immortal; what will die must be changed into what cannot die. Thanks be to God who gives us the victory through our Lord Jesus Christ (1 Corinthians 15:53, 57).

Hail, Mary, . . . the fruit of your womb, Jesus,

who makes all things new.

5. The Coronation of Our Lady and the Glory of All the Saints

A great and mysterious sight appeared in the sky. There was a woman whose dress was the sun, and who had the moon under her feet, and a crown of twelve stars on her head. She gave birth to a Son who will rule over all nations with a rod of iron (Revelation 12:1, 5).

Hail, Mary, . . . the fruit of your womb, Jesus,

who will come again in glory to judge the living and the dead.

After the Glorious Mysteries:
Regina Caeli

Joy fill your heart, O Queen most high, alleluia!
Your Son who in the tomb did lie, alleluia!
Has risen as he did prophesy, alleluia!
Pray for us, Mother, when we die, alleluia!

Rejoice and be glad, O Virgin Mary, alleluia,
—for the Lord has truly risen, alleluia.

Let us pray.

God our Father,
you give joy to the world
by the resurrection of your Son,
        our Lord Jesus Christ.
Through the prayers of his mother, the Virgin Mary,
bring us to the happiness of eternal life.
We ask this through Christ our Lord.
—Amen.

Memorare

Remember, most loving Virgin Mary,
never was it heard
that anyone who turned to you for help
was left unaided.
Inspired by this confidence,
though burdened by my sins,
I run to you for protection
for you are my mother.
Mother of the Word of God,
do not despise my words of pleading
but be merciful and hear my prayer.
Amen.

Text: Claude Bernard (1588-1641) was the popularizer of the 16th century version of this 15th century prayer. *A Book of Prayers* (Washington D.C.: ICEL, 1982), p. 34.

12. To Conclude

The Lord's Prayer Paraphrased

Our Father in heaven—
> Abba, dear father,
> you live and reign in heaven,
> our Creator, Maker and Sustainer.

Hallowed be your name—
> Your name is holy above all other names
> and must be venerated above all other names
> especially by me your child of grace.
> May I live and act so as to hallow your name
> in the sight of all.

Your kingdom come—
> May your kingdom be my life's center,
> the principal point of my desires.
> Let it be to me a state of grace here and now
> and a state of glory in the world to come.

Your will be done, on earth as in heaven—
    Let self-will depart from me.
    Let your holy and gracious will
    be done in me and by me,
    as it is in heaven by saints and angels.

Give us today our daily bread—
    Give me what I need for health and peace.
    Fix my heart on things above, not on things
        on earth.
    Give me the bread from heaven for my salvation.

Forgive us our sins—
    Forgive me my debts, the huge sum I owe you,
    shameful falls, frequent relapses, daily wallowings.
    With God there is mercy and plenteous redemption.

As we forgive those who sin against us—
    Help me to love my enemies
    and pray for those who mistreat and persecute me.
    Teach me to forgive as I am forgiven.

Save us from the time of trial—
    Mindful of my frailty,
    save me from trial and temptation
    and be my Savior on the great and final day

And deliver us from evil—
>From the world, the flesh and the devil.
>From the evils of the present age
>>and of the age to come.
>From the evils of punishment which we so
>>richly deserve.
>From all evils, past, present and future.
>From all these deliver me, good Lord.
>For the kingdom, the power and the glory are
>>yours, now and for ever. Amen.

Text: Bishop Lancelot Andrewes (1555-1626), alt.

Acknowledgments

The publisher gratefully acknowledges the following sources from which portions of this book were compiled:

American Bible Society. *The Good News Bible. Today's English Version (TEV).* © American Bible Society second ed. 1992. Reprinted by permission. Unless otherwise indicated, scriptural passages are from *The Good News Bible, TEV.*

Cambridge University Press. *The New English Bible.* © 1970. The delegates of the Oxford University Press and the Syndics of the Cambridge University Press 1961, 1970 for six short New Testament passages. Reprinted by permission.

Division of Christian Education of the National Council of churches in the U.S.A. *New Revised Standard Version,* © 1993 and 1989.

International Committee on English in the Liturgy, Inc. The Alternative Opening Prayer and the English translation of the Opening Prayer from *The Roman Missal* © 1973, International Committee on English in the Liturgy, Inc. (ICEL); excerpts from the English translation of the Prayer after Mass, *Memorare*, Prayer of Self-Dedication to Christ, and the Litanies of St. Joseph, Loreto, the Sacred Heart, and the Holy Name from *A Book of Prayers* © 1982,

Charles M. Guilbert, Custodian. *Prayers, Thanksgivings and Litanies.* © 1973 for "For the Church," "For Families," and "Prayer to the Holy Spirit."

Charles M. Guilbert, Custodian. *The Book of Common Prayer.* © 1977 for "Christ Our Passover."

Harper & Row, Publishers. *Prayers for Help and Healing* by William Barclay. © 1968 for "A Night Prayer For Those in Need."

Oxford University Press, Inc. *Poems of Gerard Manley Hopkins,* Fourth Edition, ed. W. H. Gardner and N. H. MacKenzie. © 1967. The Society of Jesus for "Jesu Dulcis Memoria," "Adoro Te Devote" (St. Thomas Aquinas), "To Jesus Living in Mary" (Fr. Charles de Condren), and "O God I Love Thee" (St. Francis Xavier).

Paulist Press. *Francis and Clare, The Complete Works,* edited and translated by Regis Armstrong, O.F.M. Cap. and Ignatius C. Brady, O.F.M., © 1982 For "Salutation to the Blessed Virgin Mary."

_____. *Christopher Prayers for Today* by Richard Armstrong. © 1972 for "For Brotherhood," "For God's Good Earth," and "An Easter Prayer."

_____. *Prayer for Each Day* by Jose Feder. © 1974. The Missionary Society of St. Paul the Apostle in the State of New York for "For a Holy Heart," "For Those We Love," "For the Needy," "Now Let Me Accept," "Raise Me Up, Lord," and "Prayer to Mary for the Sick."

_____. *Showings* by Julian of Norwich, translated by Colledge-Walsh. © 1978 for two selections.

The following prayers are original compositions of William
G. Storey, © 1978, 2000 by Ave Maria Press, all rights reserved:
"Litany to the Holy Spirit," "For Love and Service," "Lord Jesus,
Healer," "Litany of the Faithful Departed," "Litany of the
Blessed Sacrament of the Altar," "Litany to the Spirit of the
Seven Gifts," "Litany to Christ Our Lord."

List of Prayers,
Psalms, Canticles . . .

Everyday Prayers

Prayers for All Seasons
Prayers From the Heart

Prayers for Light

Prayers for the Church

Prayers for Strength

Prayers Near Journey's End

Various Other Prayers

Psalms

Biblical Canticles

Hymns

Te Deum Laudamus/ 20, 249
    You are God: we praise you
Maria Aurora/ 181
Veni, Creator Spiritus/ 113, 260
    O Holy Spirit
Te Deum Laudamus, part B/ 219
    You, Christ are the king of glory
Marian Anthem for Advent/ 206
    Alma Redemptoris Mater
Marian Anthem for Christmastide/ 221
Marian Anthem for Lent/ 240
Christ is Risen/ 252
    St. Hippolytus
Easter Anthem/ 254
    Christ Our Passover
A Marian Anthem Throughout the Year/ 268
Salve Regina/ 374

Poems

Litanies

Eucharistic Devotions